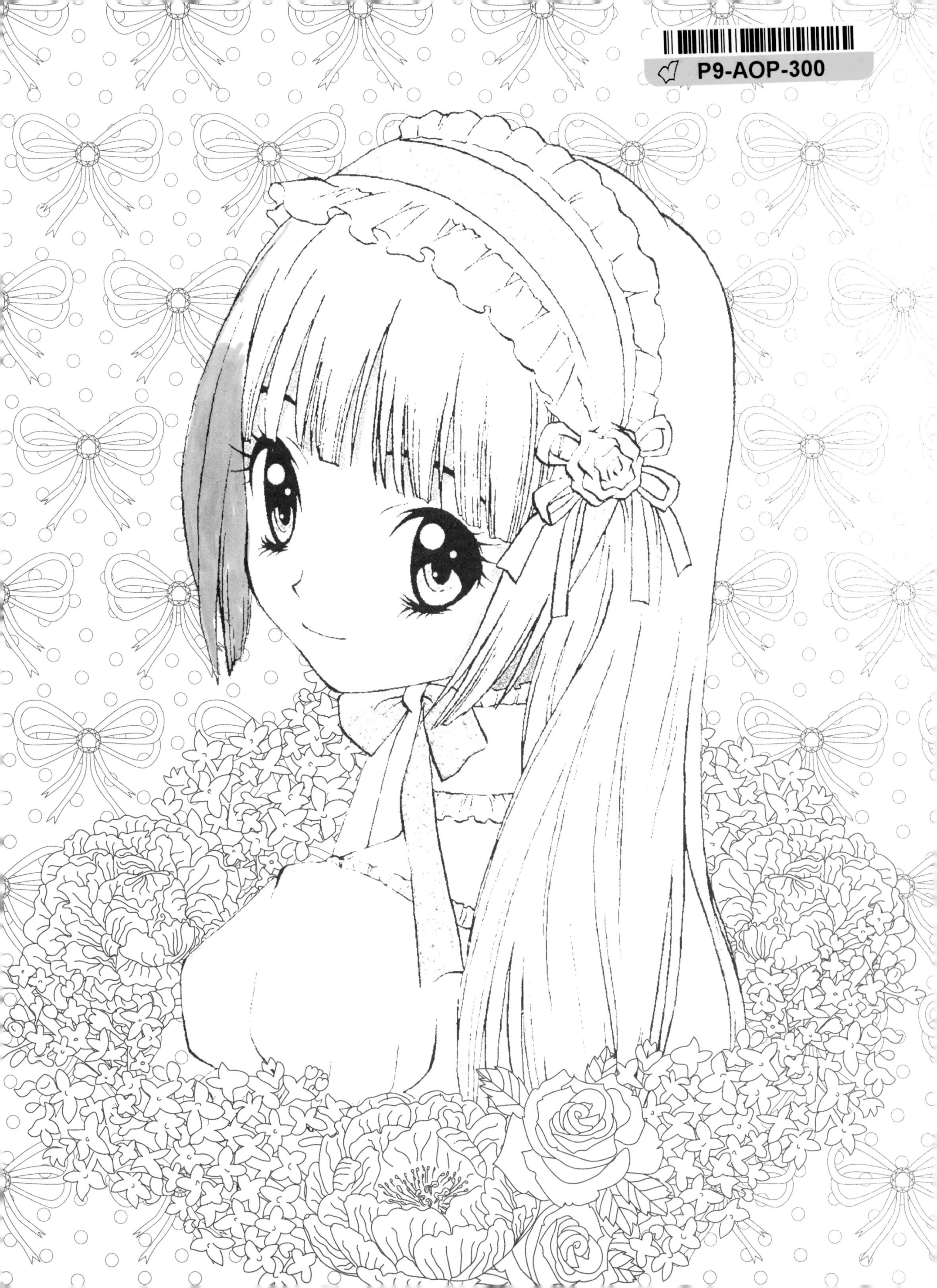

DRAWING WITH Christopher Hart

The Manga Artist's Coloring Book

GIRLS!

Fun Female Characters to Color

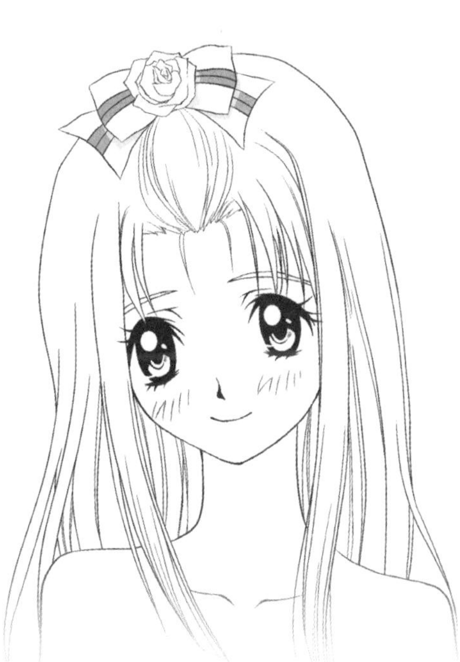

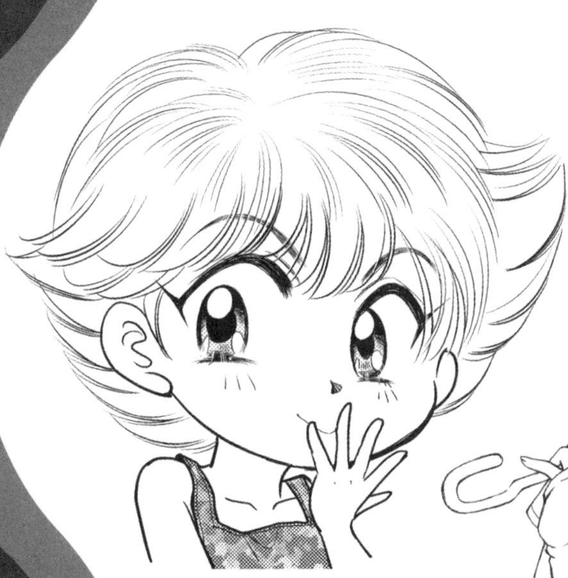

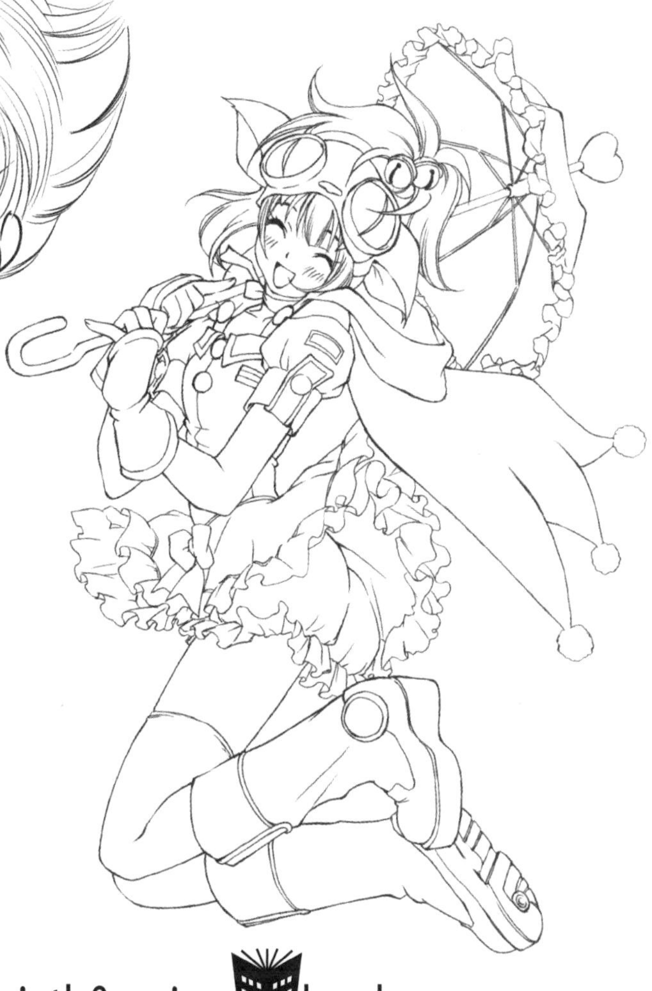

sixth&spring books
19 West 21st Street, Suite 601, New York, NY 10010

Printed in Turkey

14

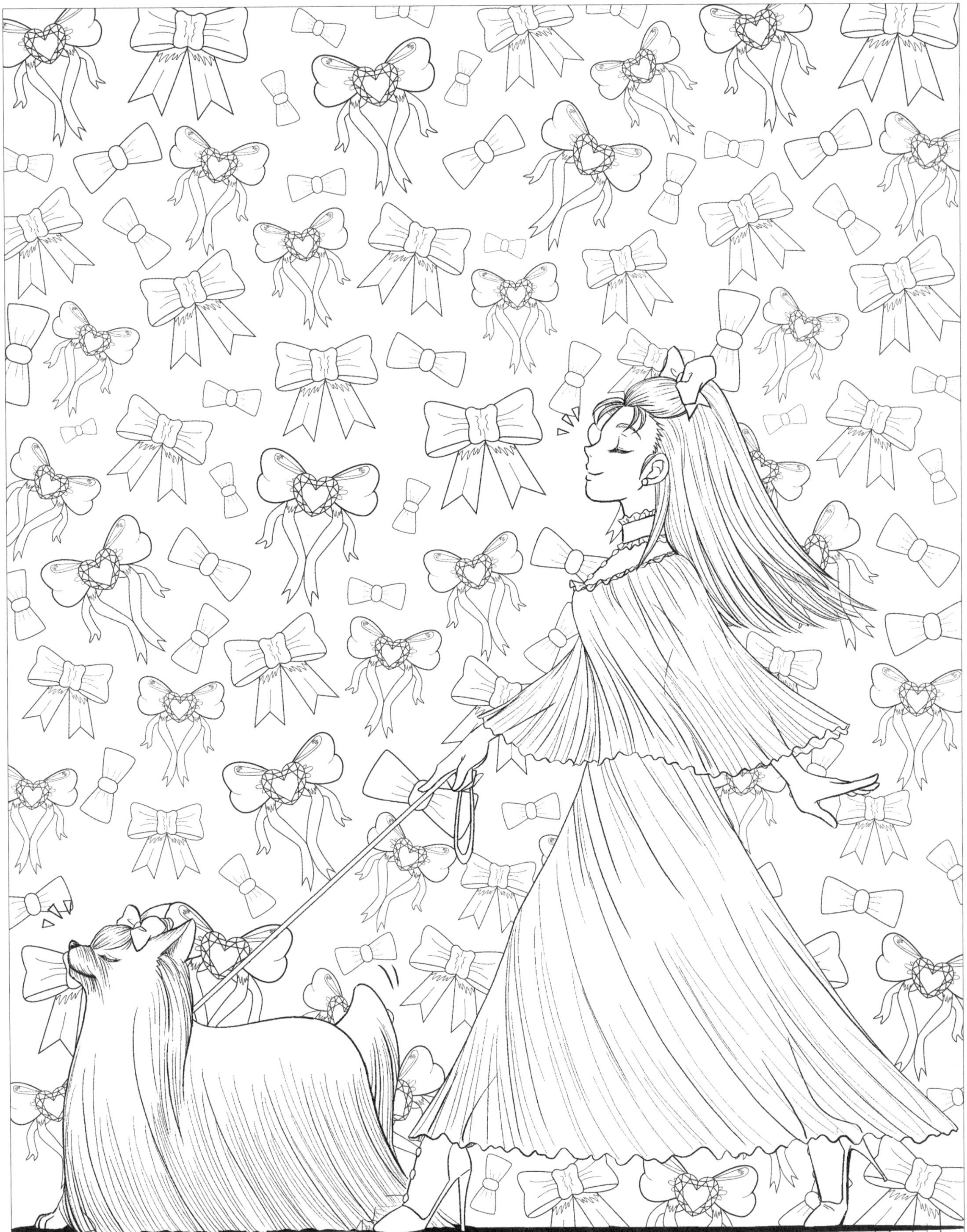

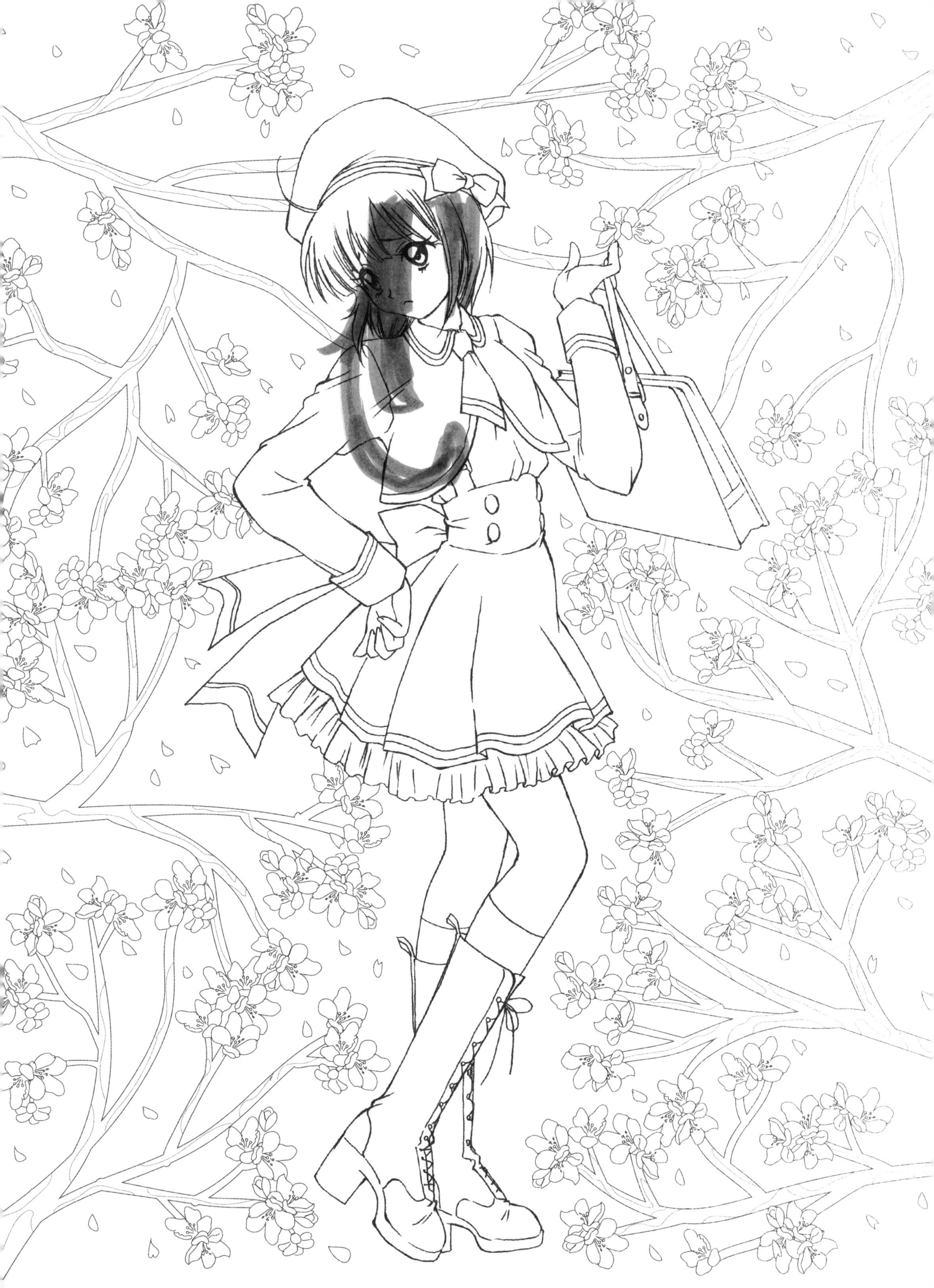

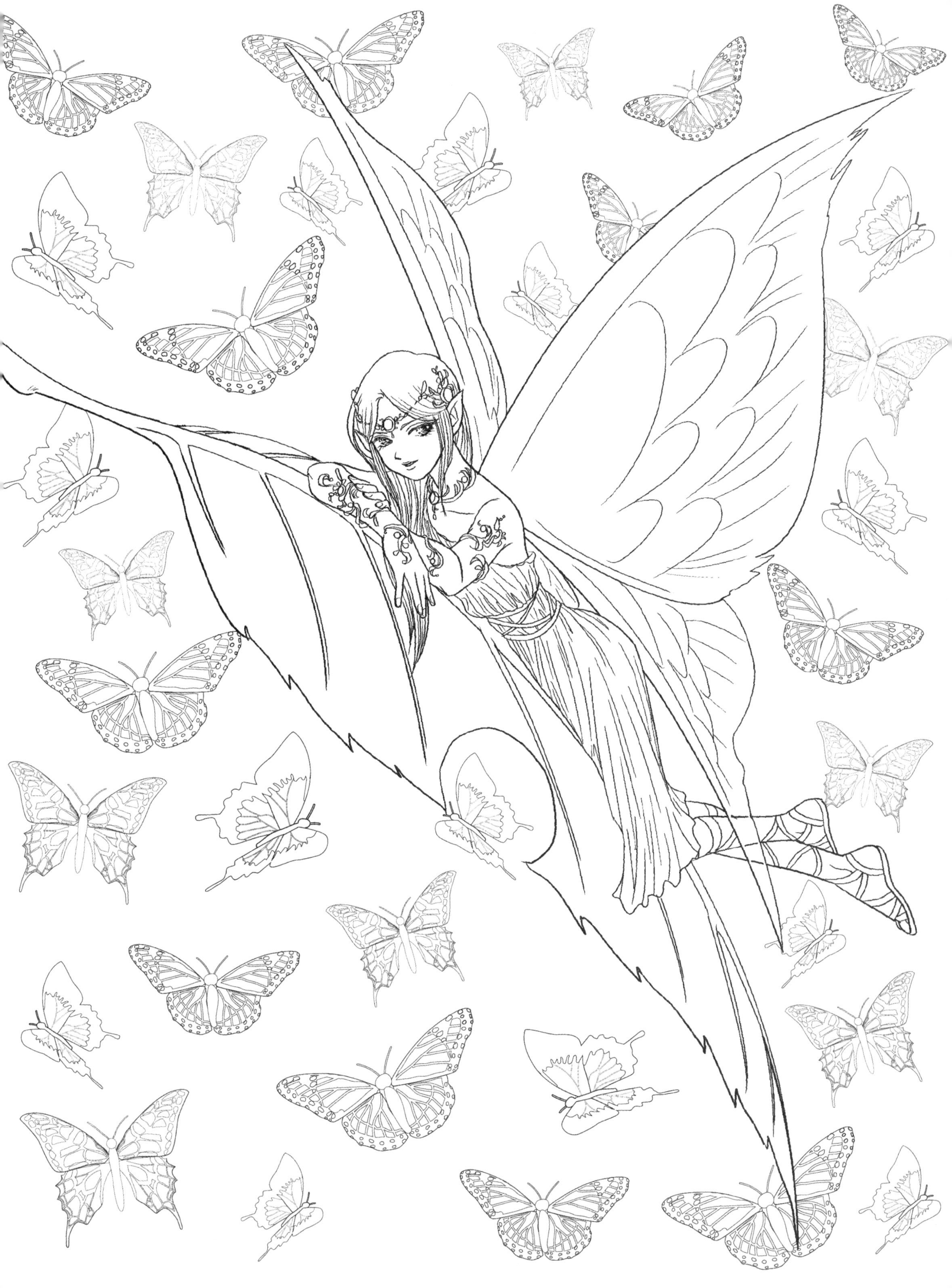

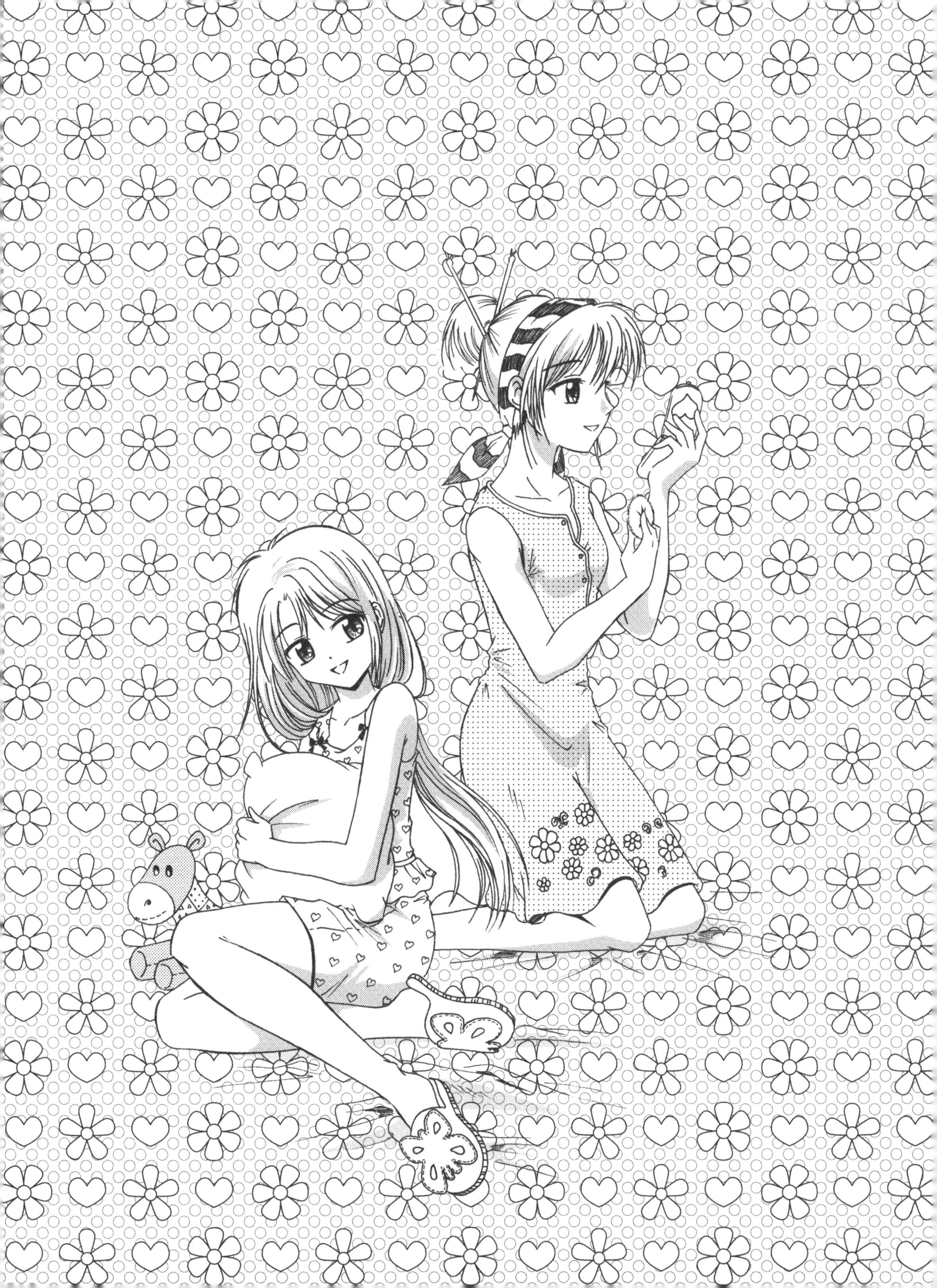

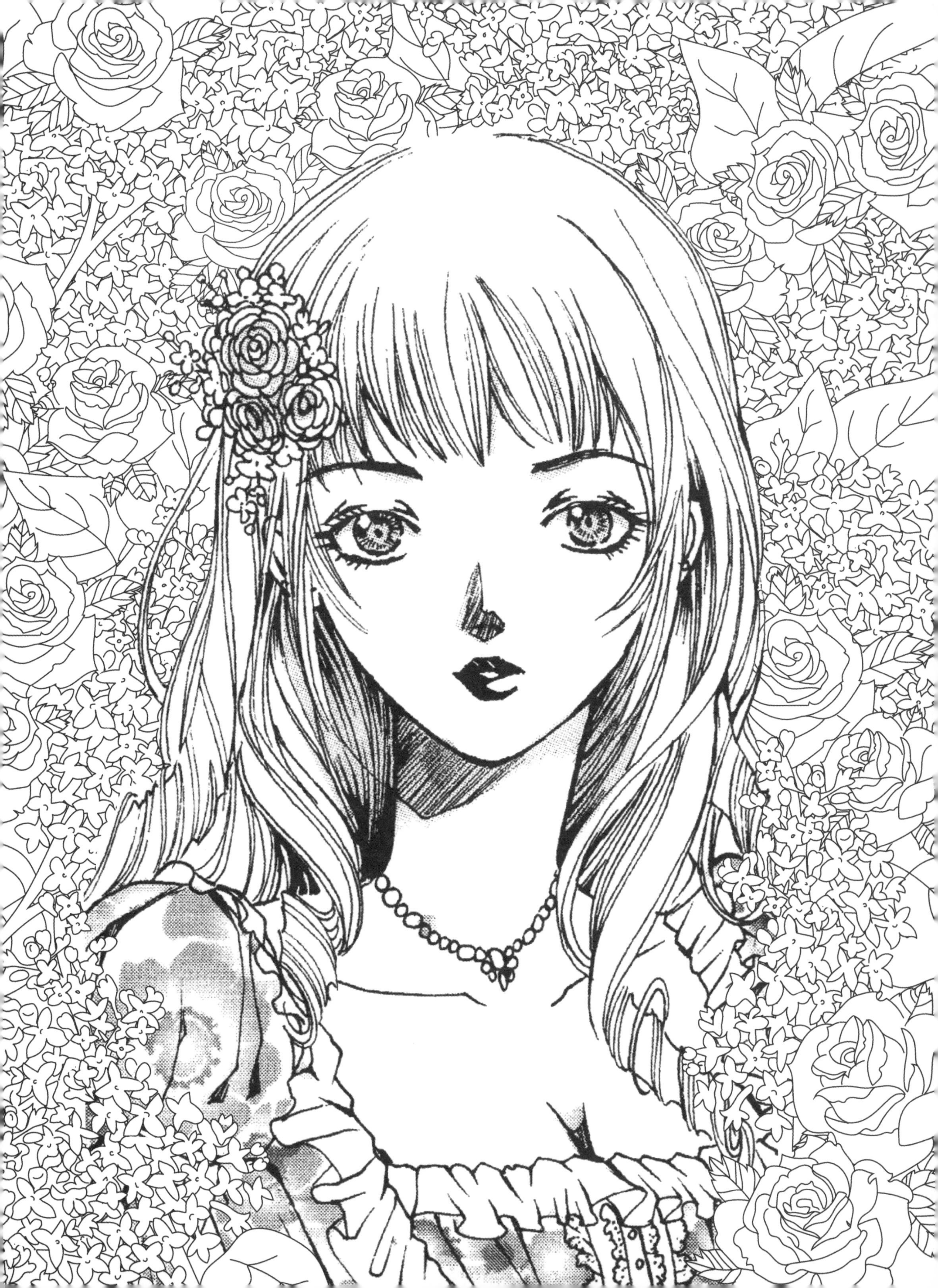

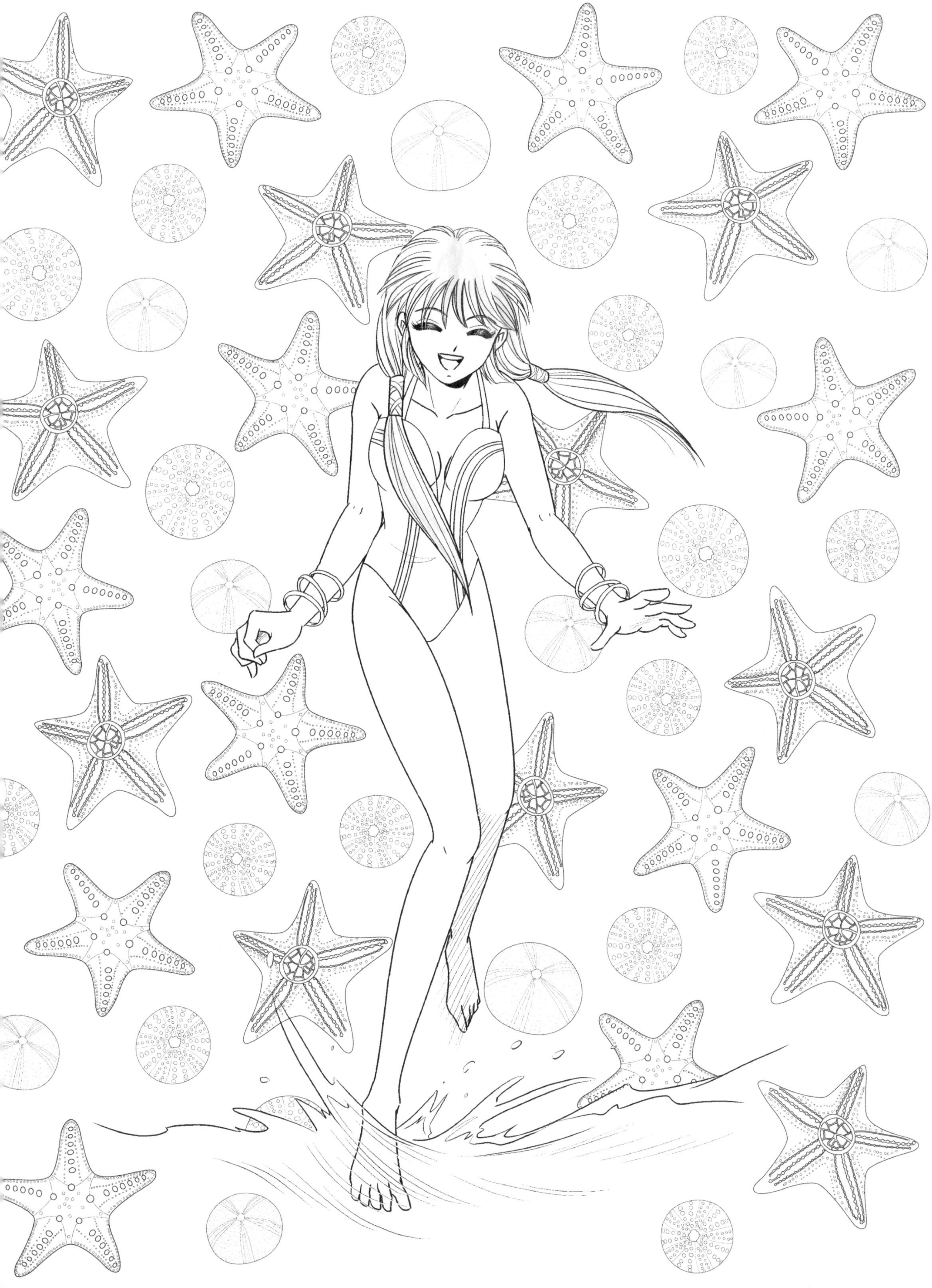

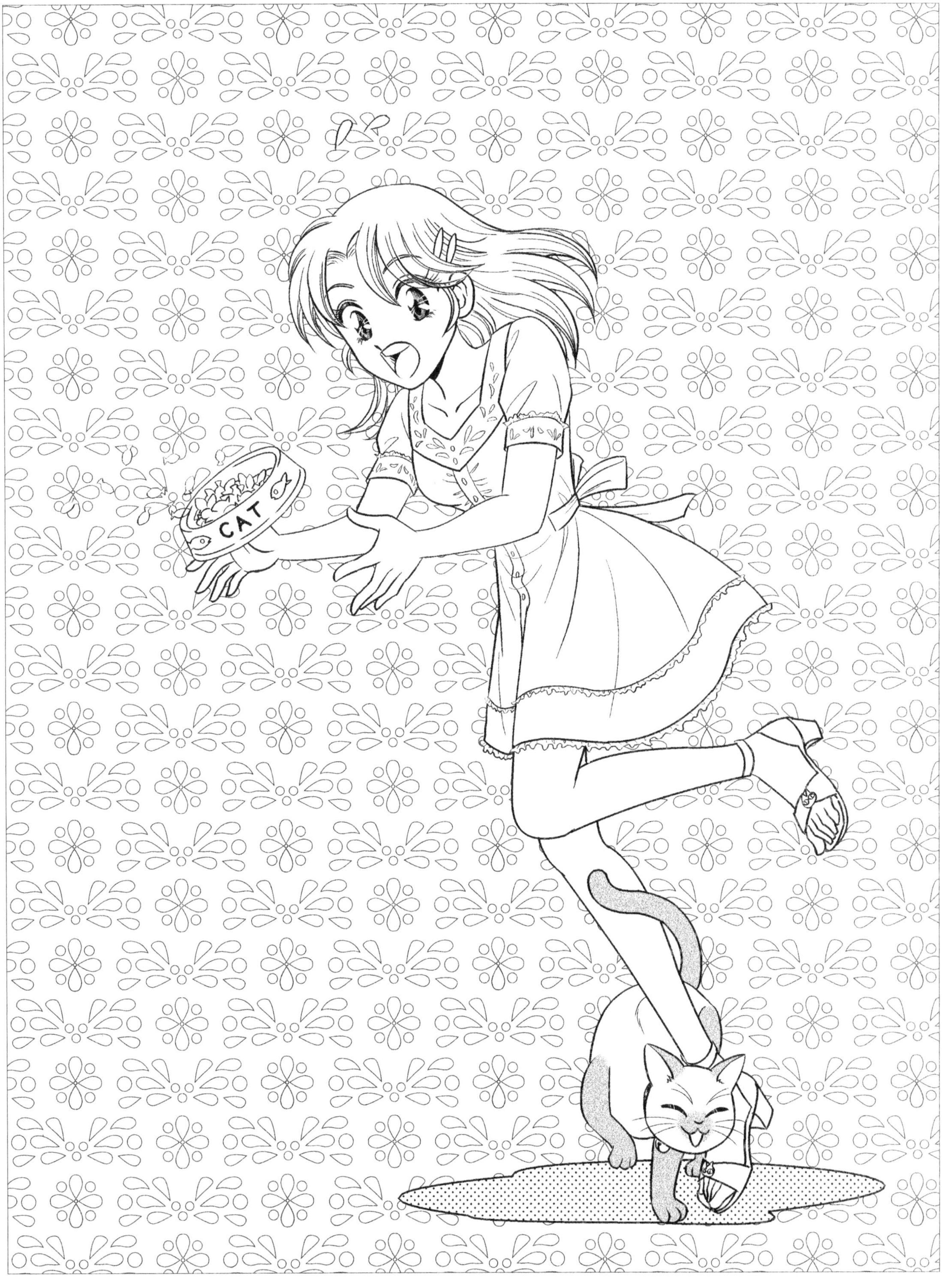
CAT

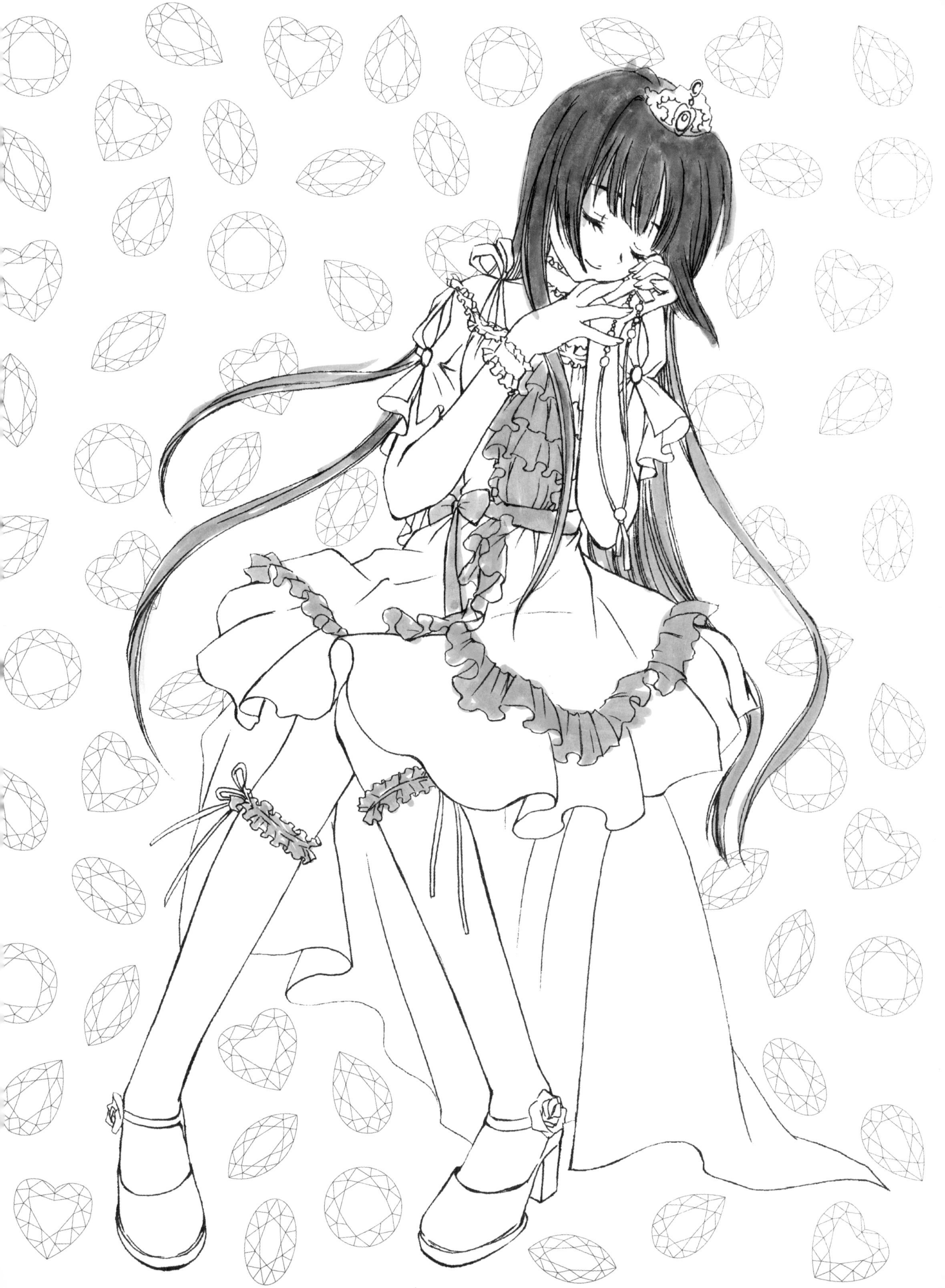

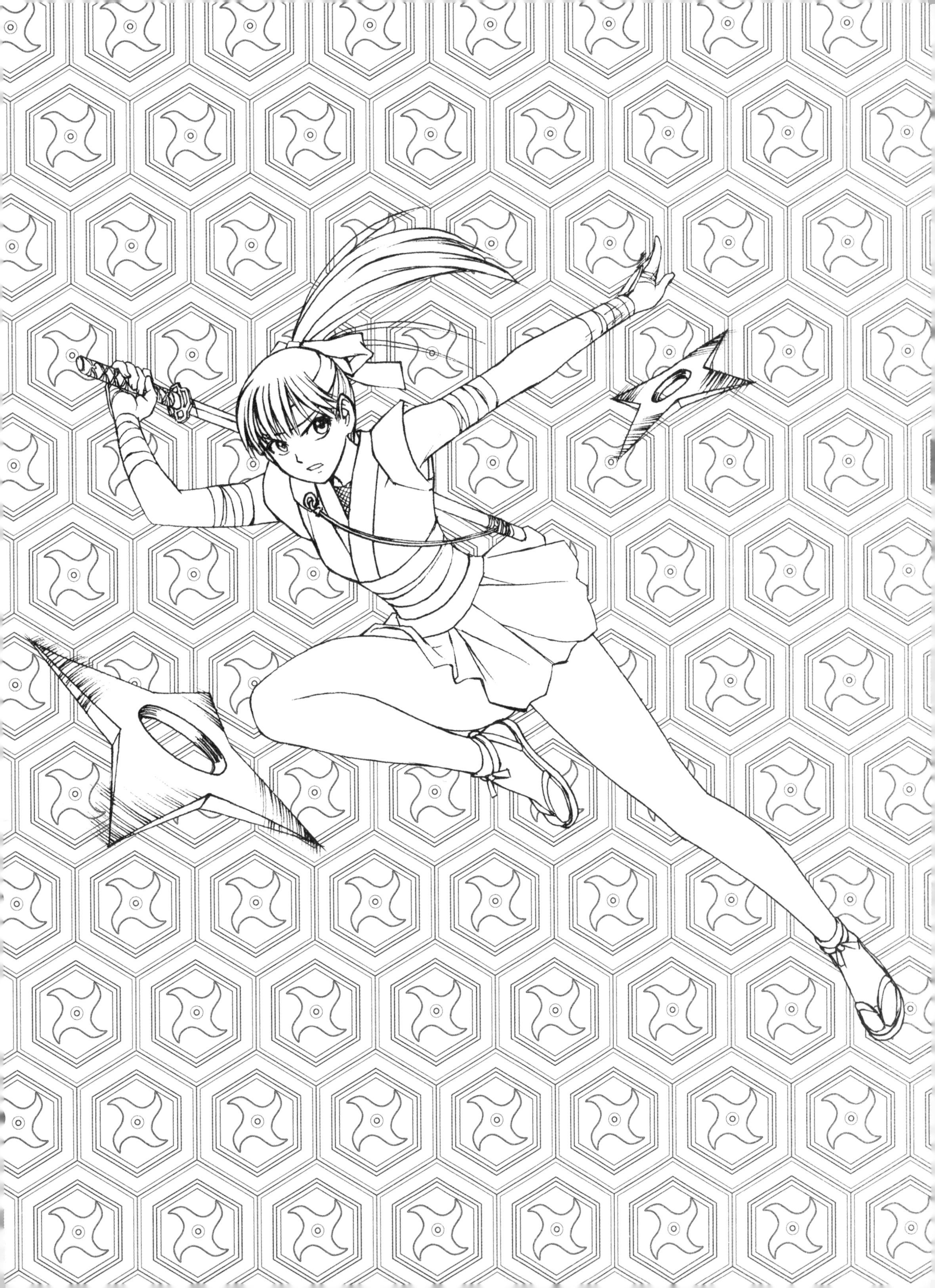

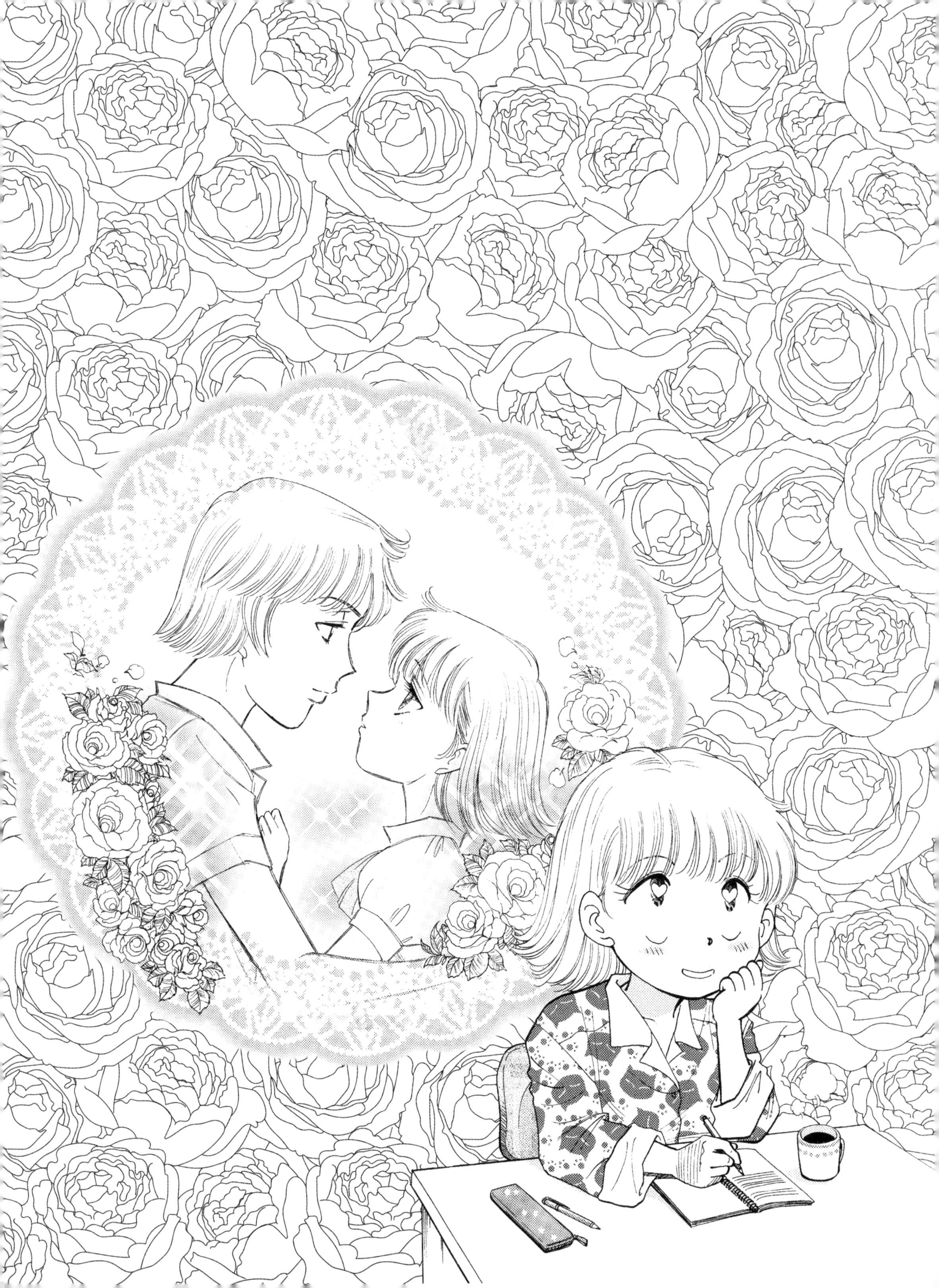

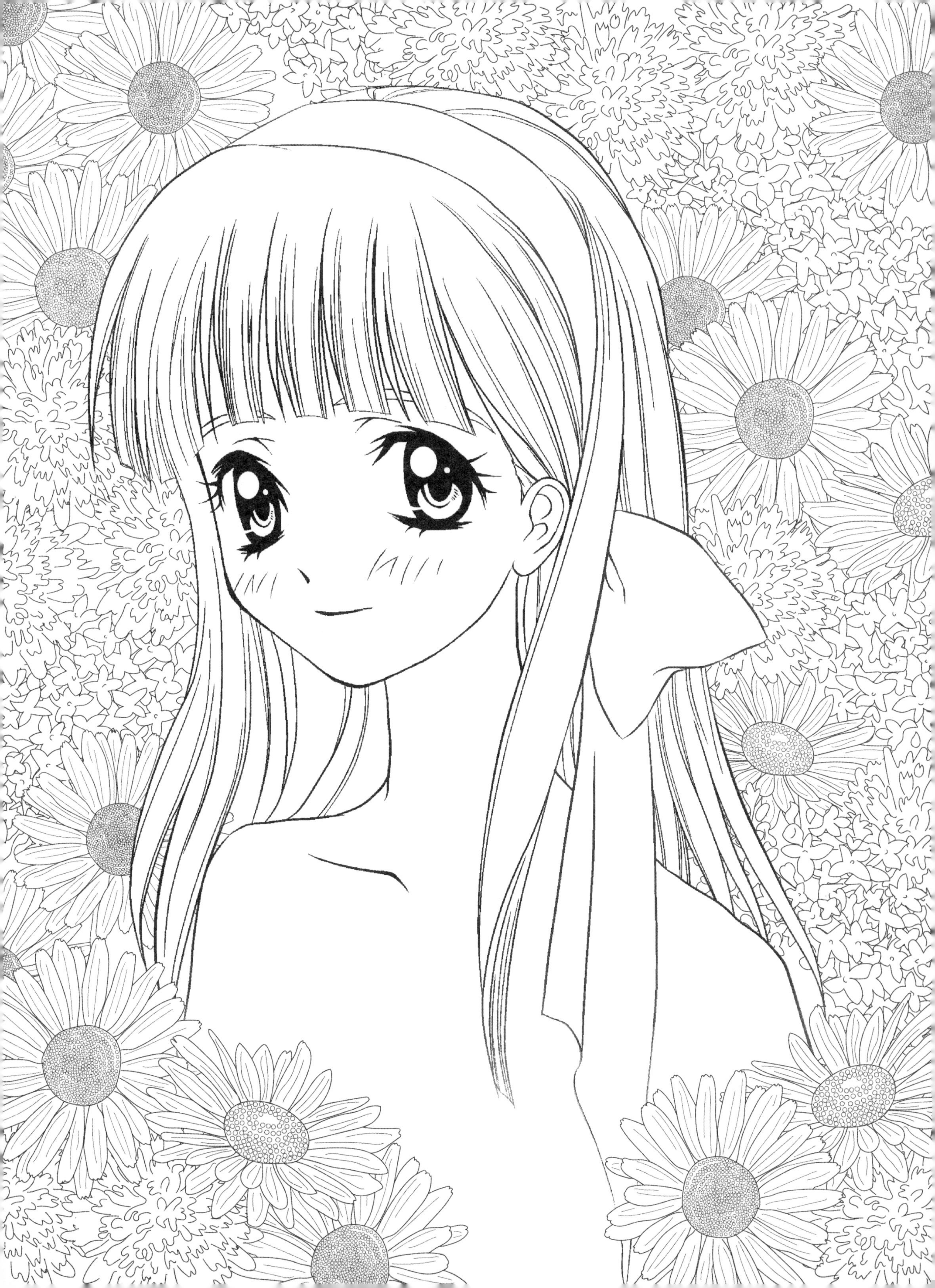

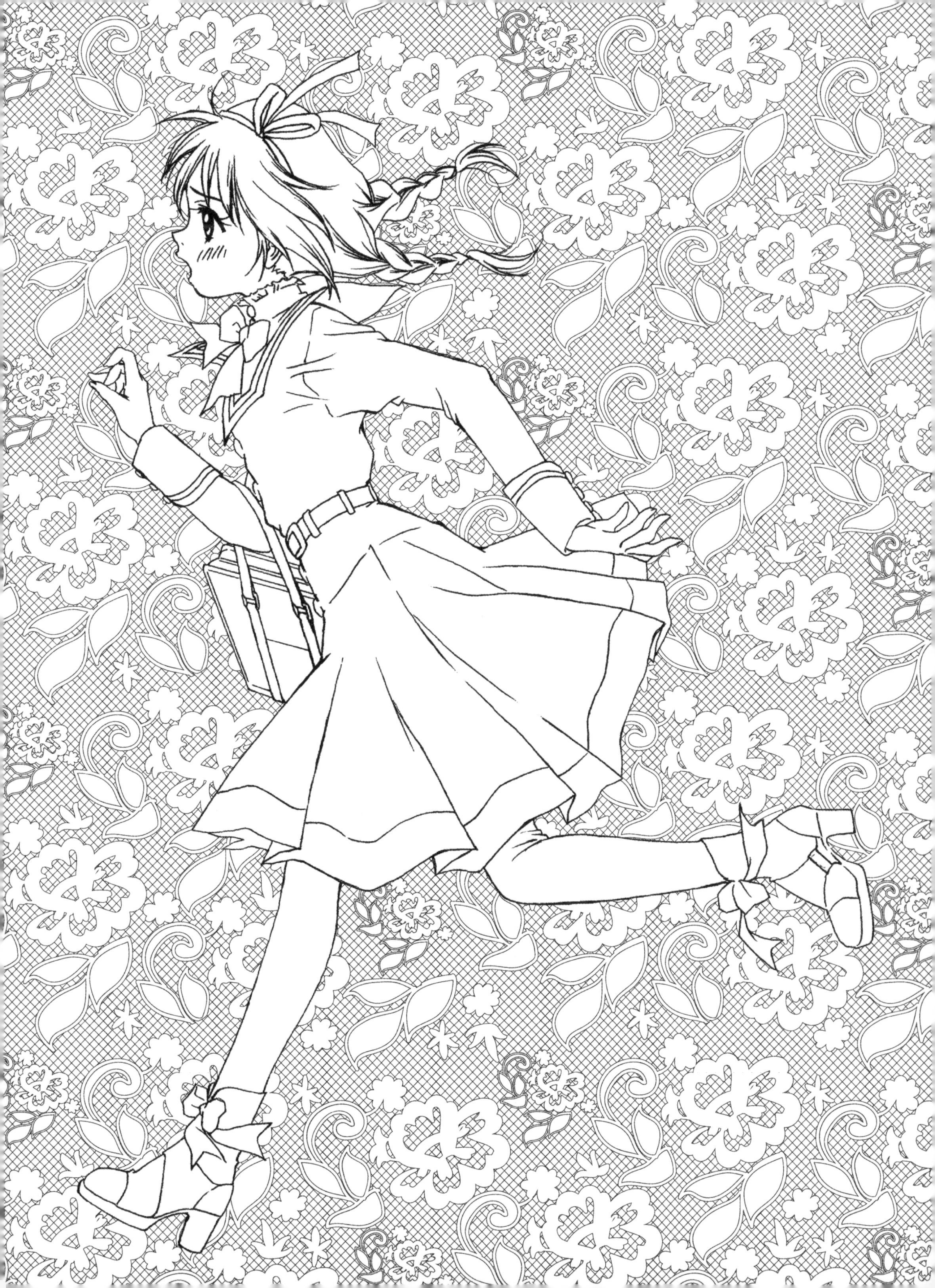

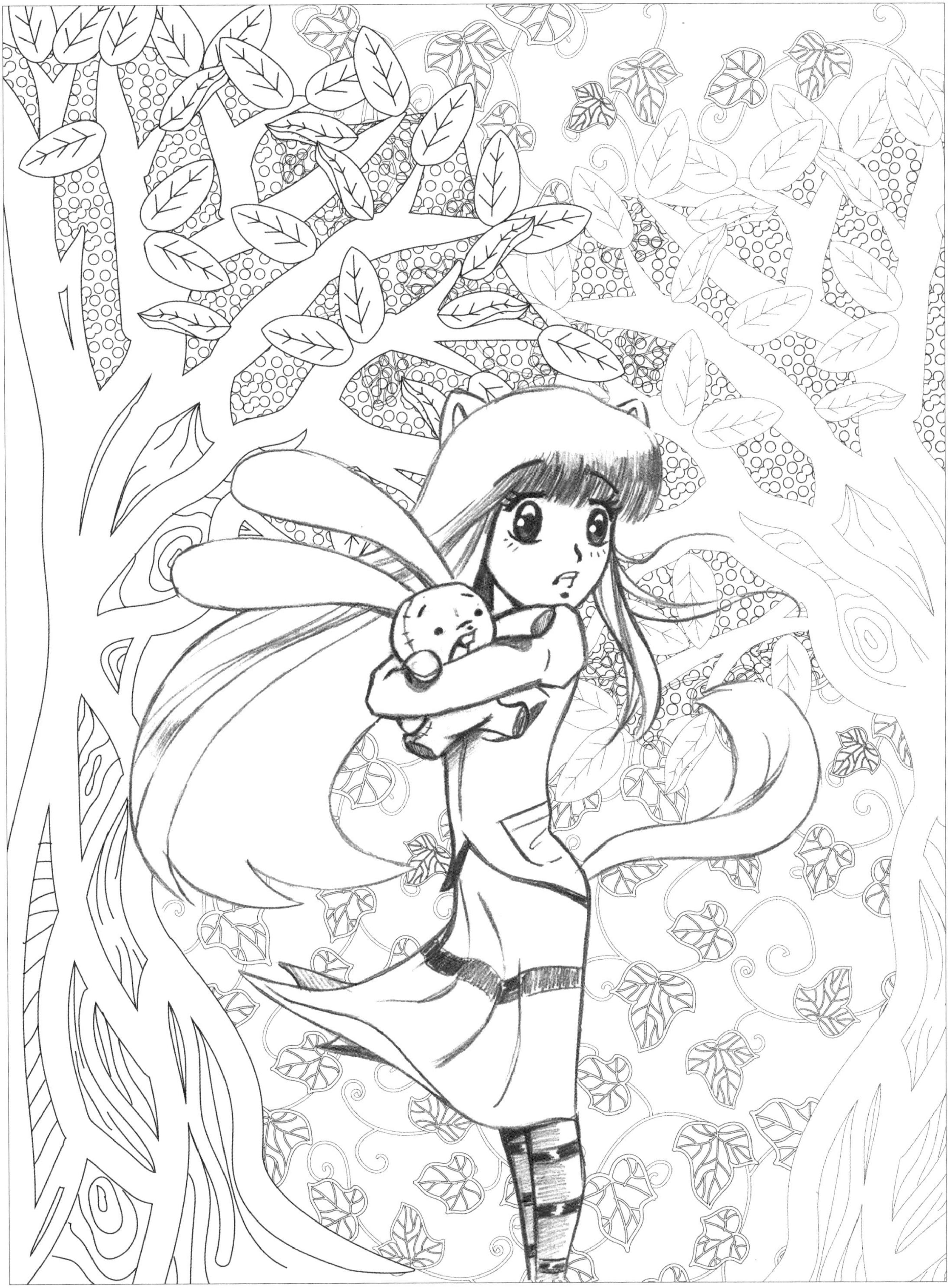

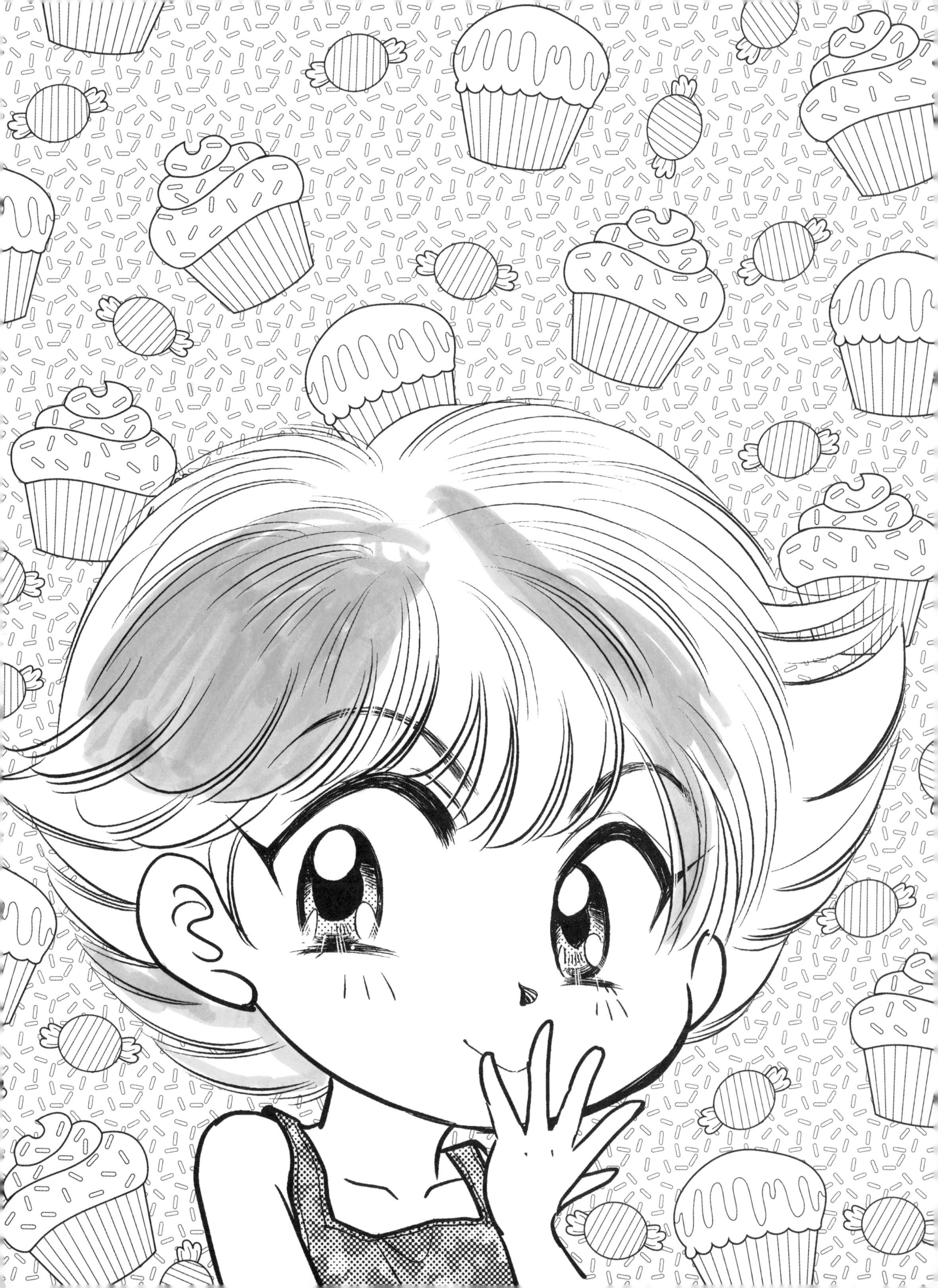

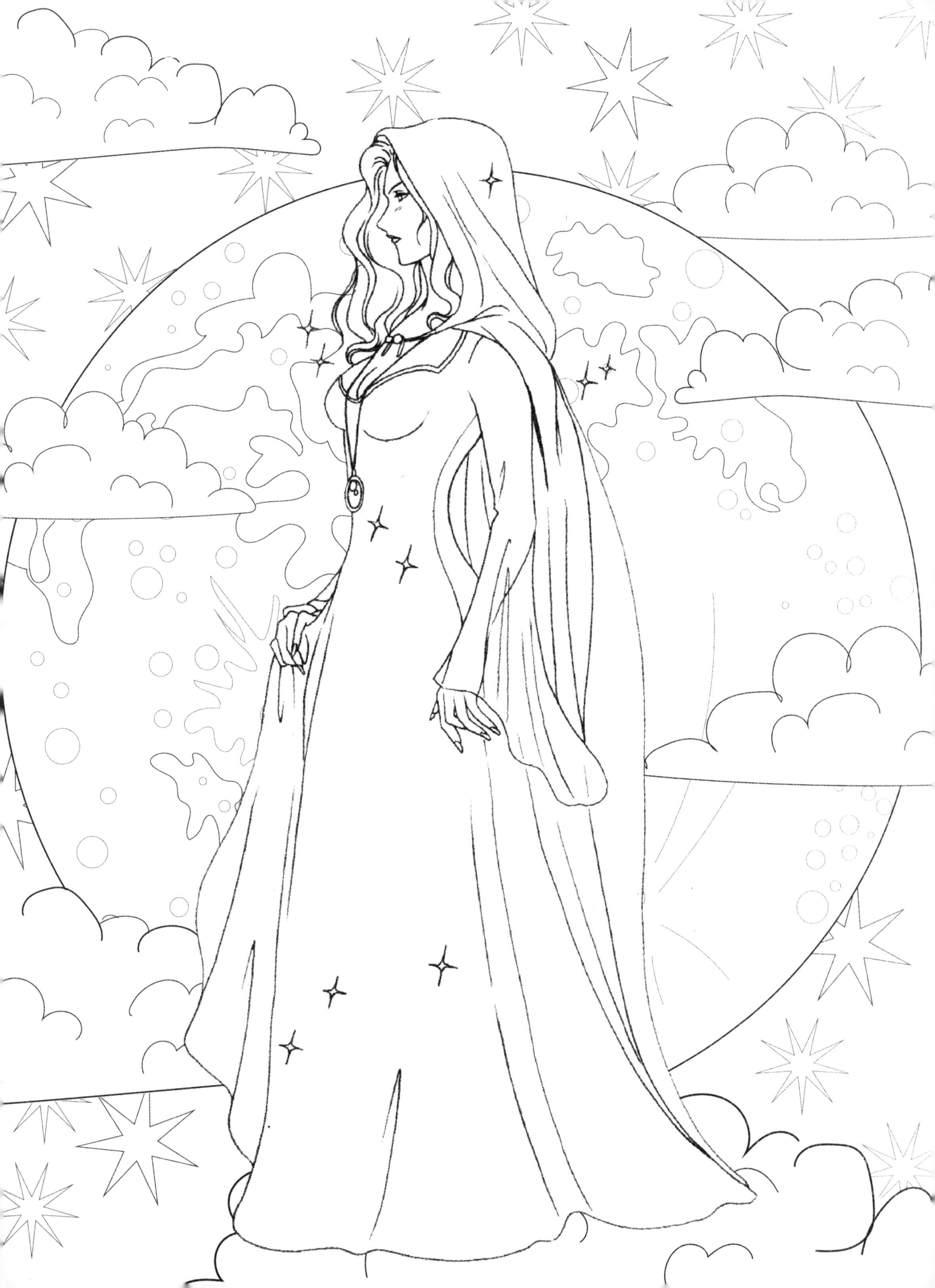

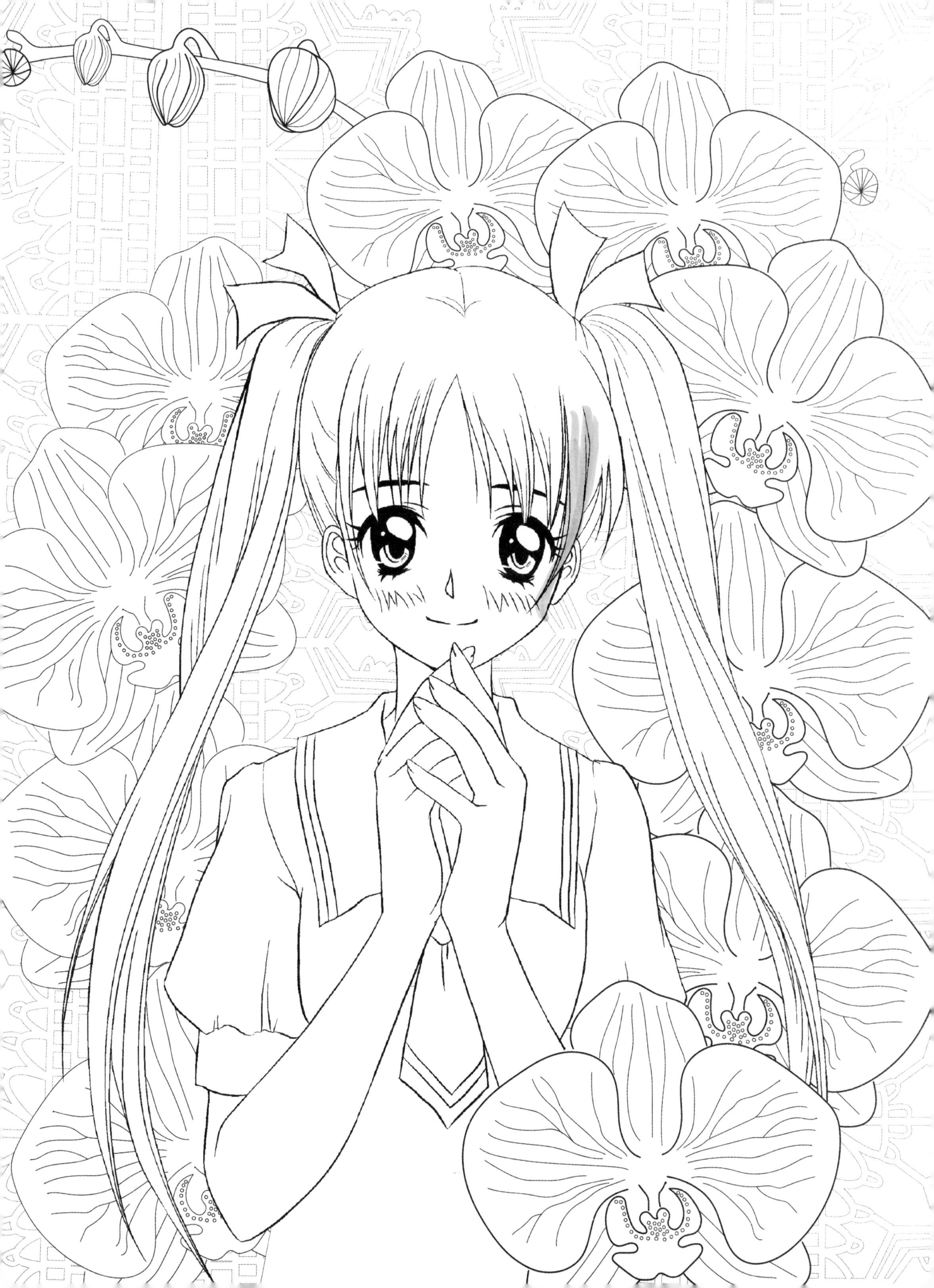

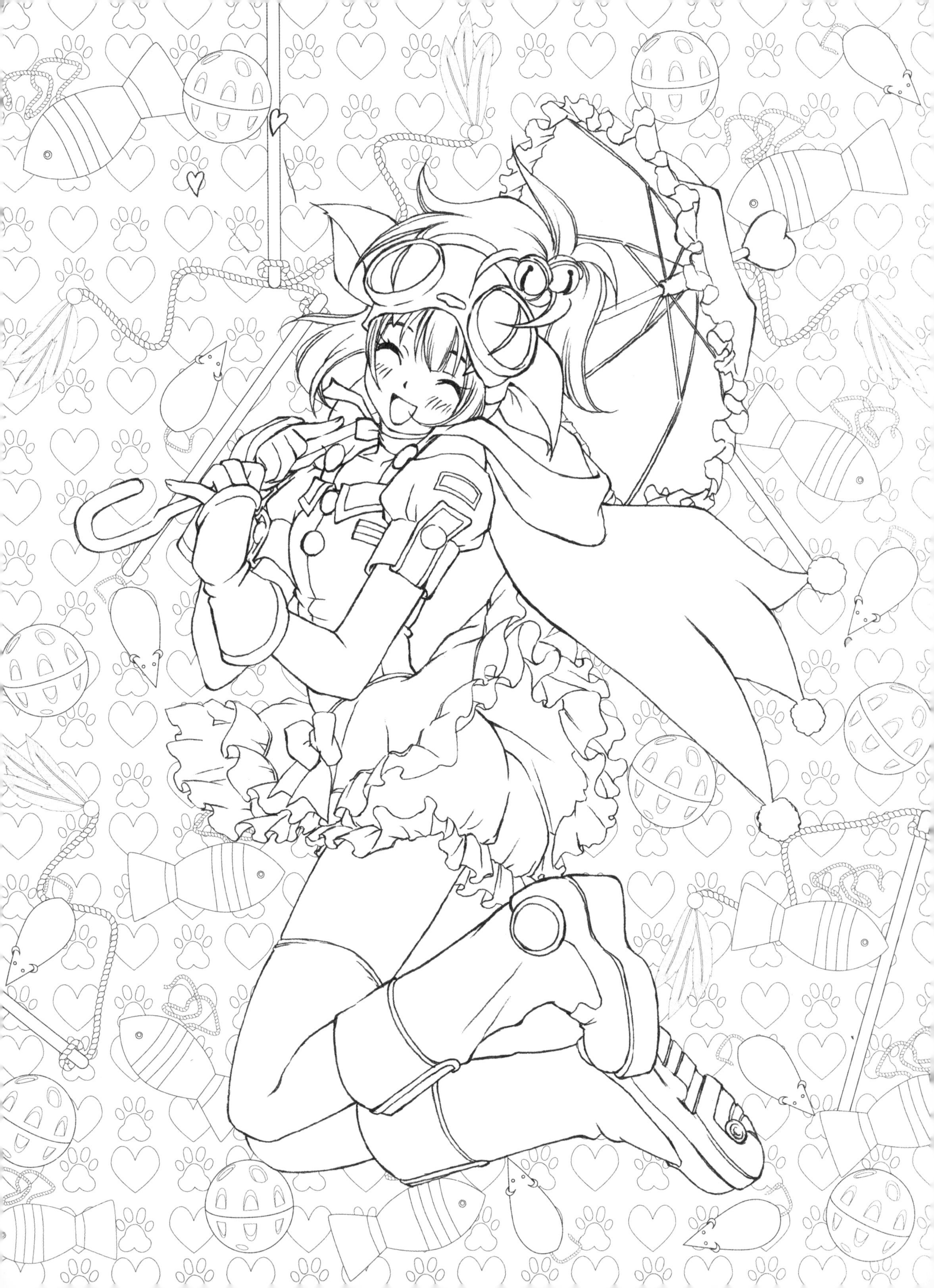

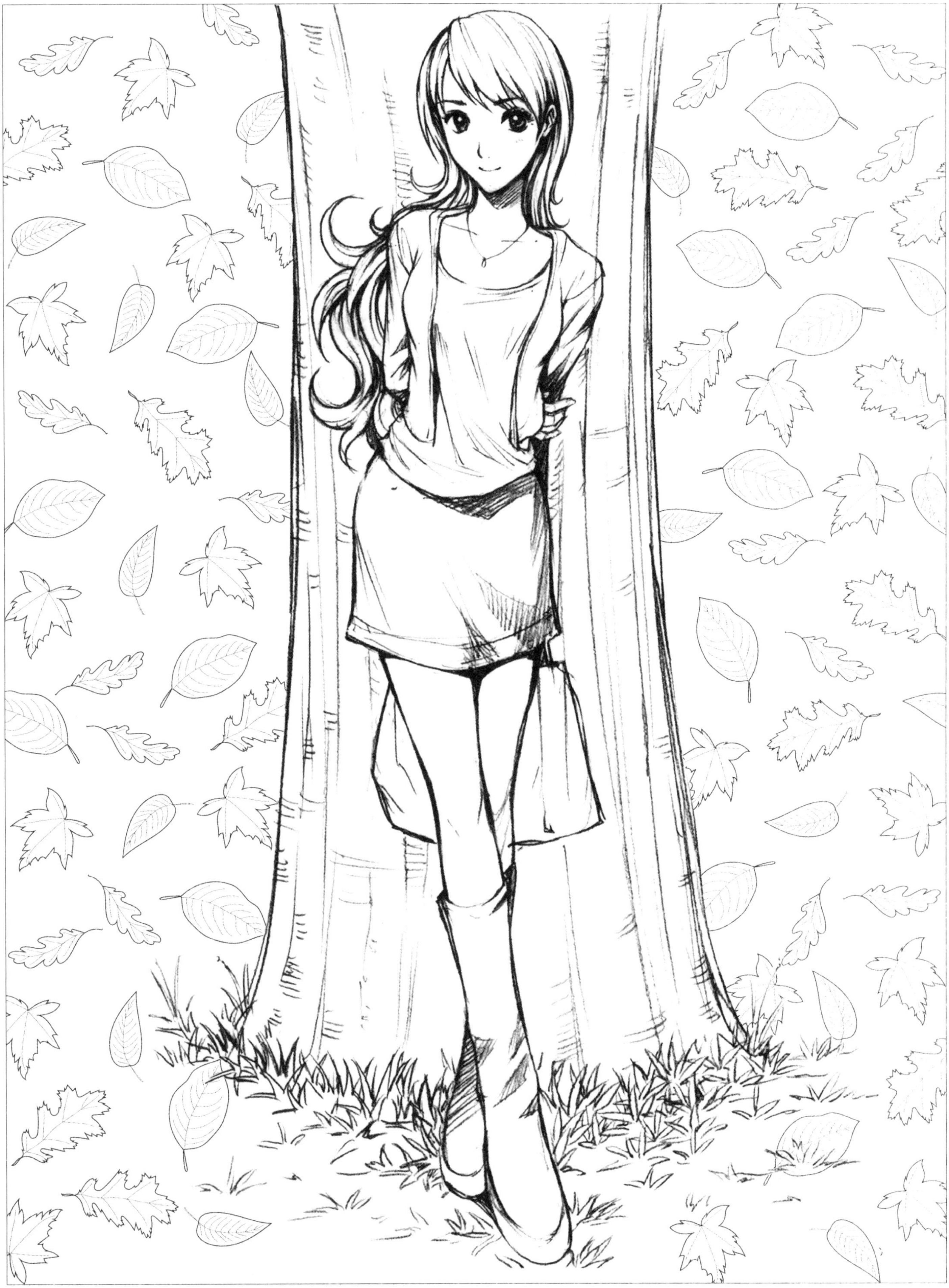

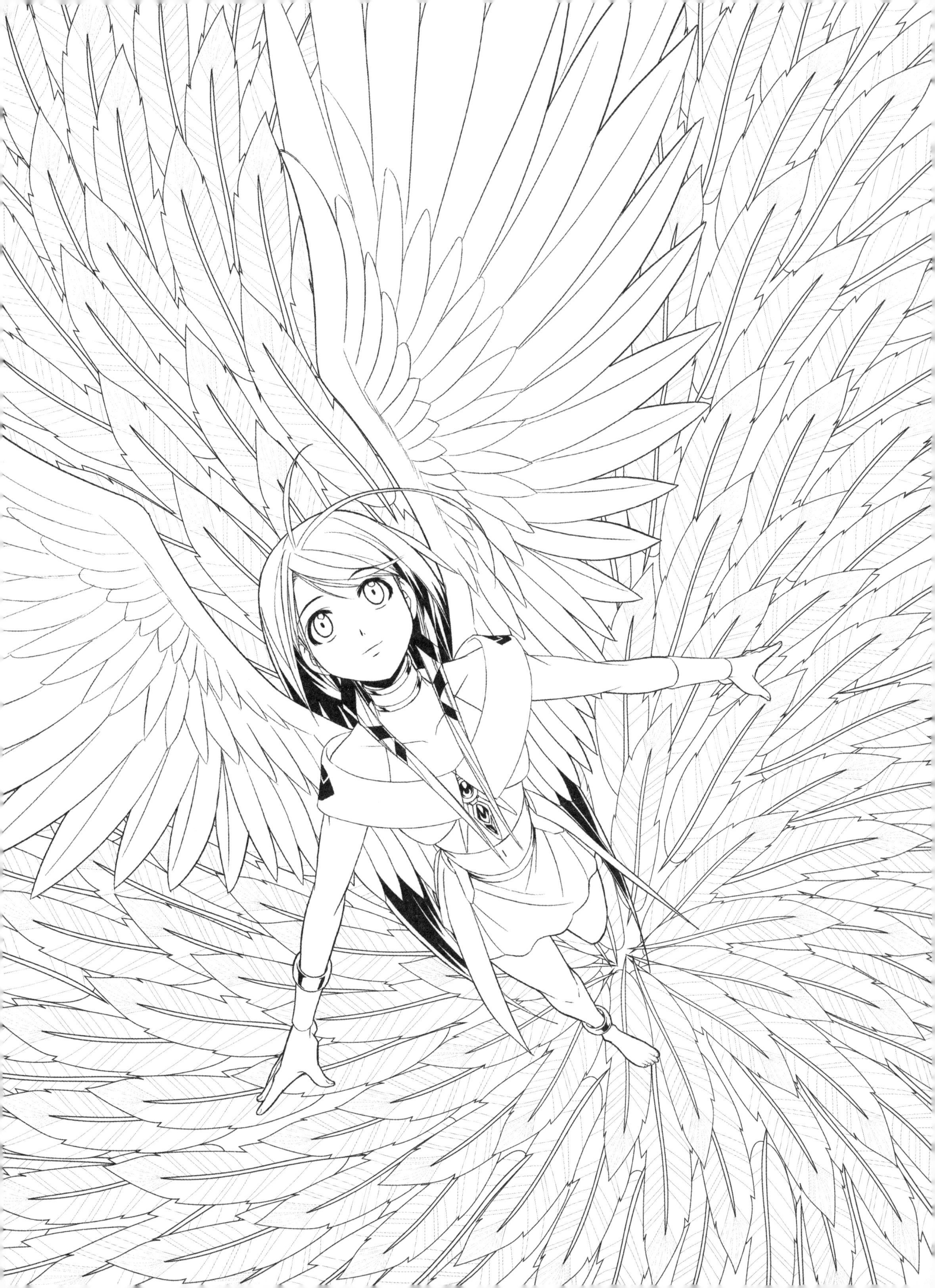

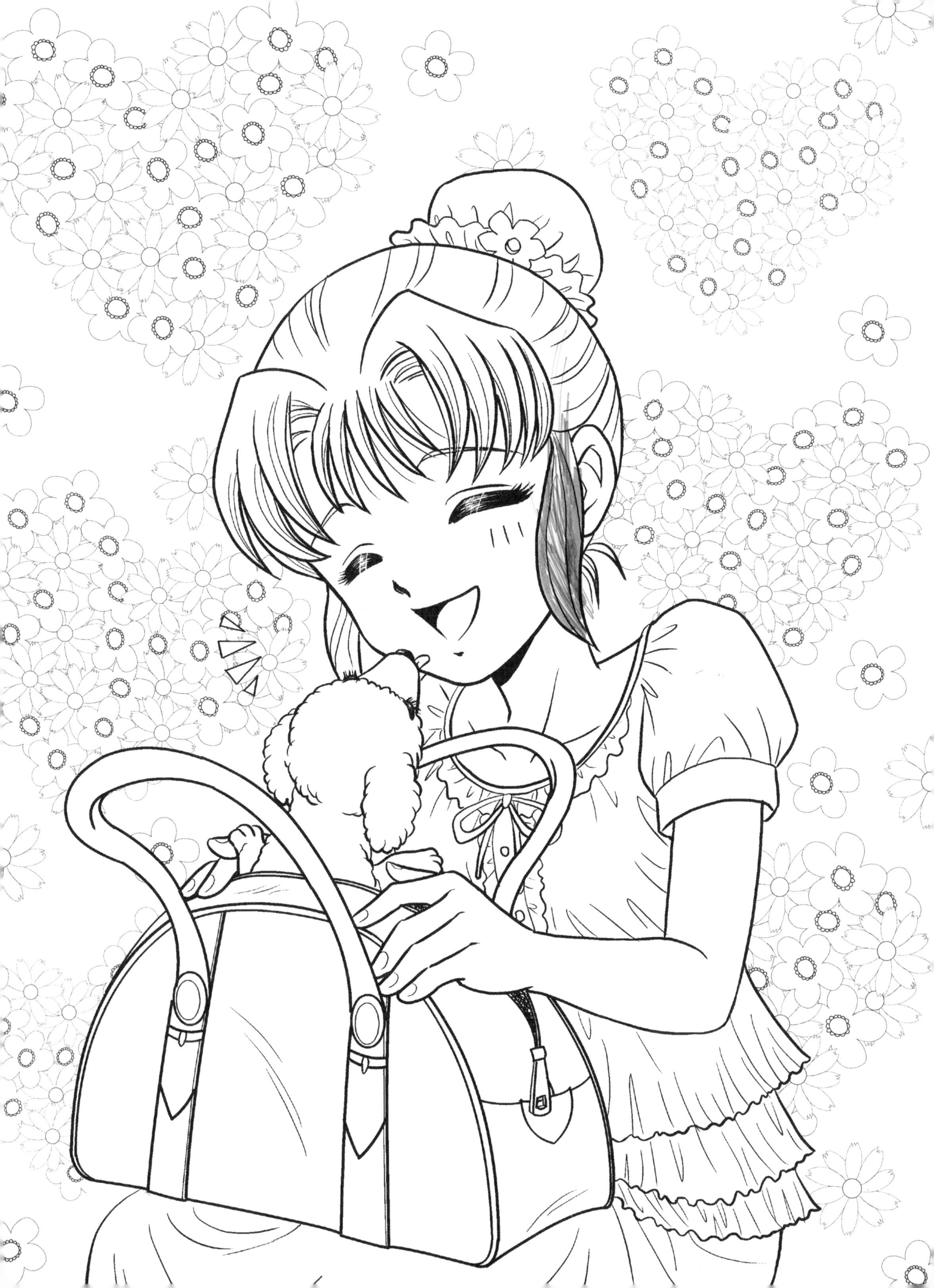

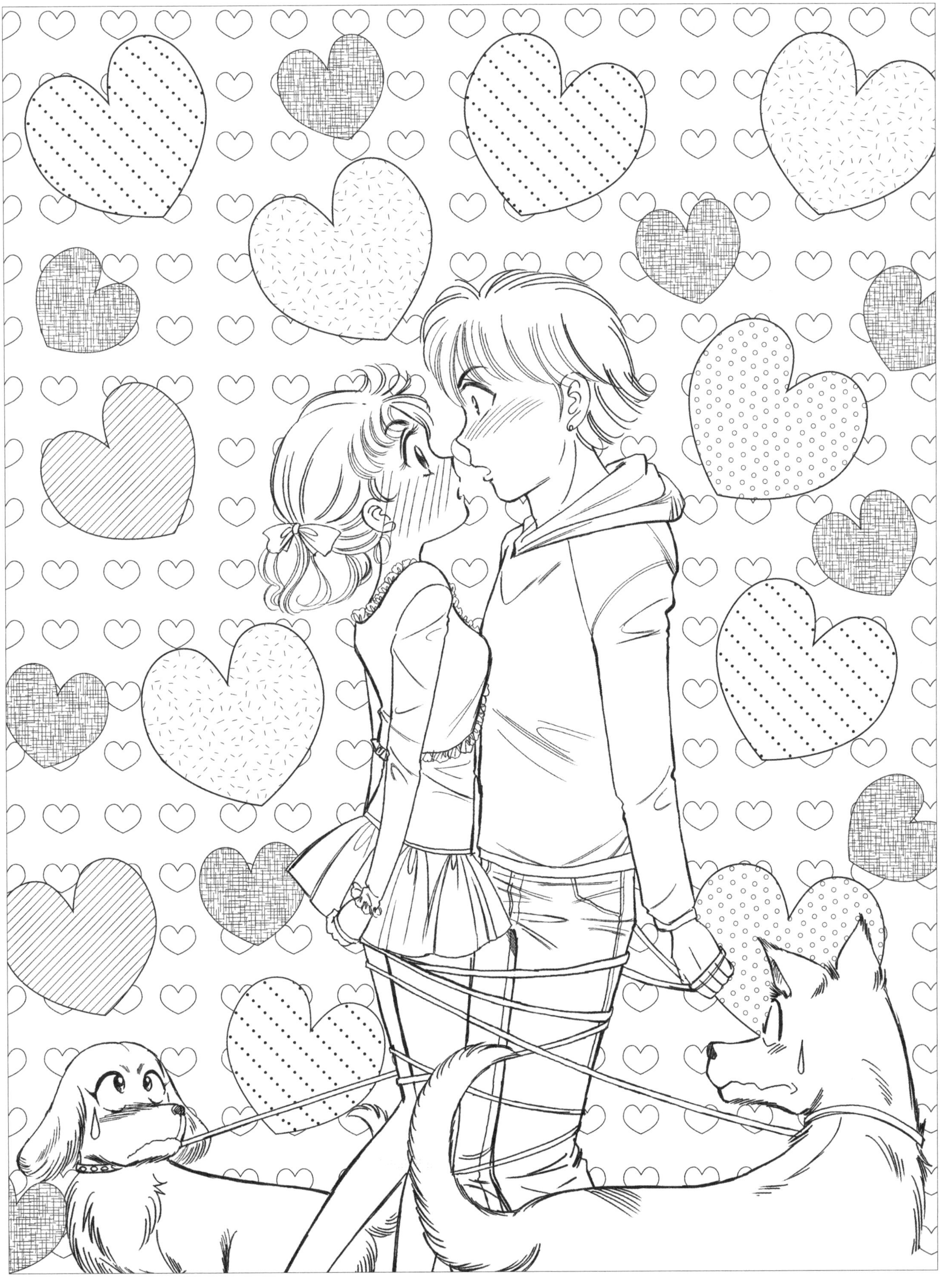

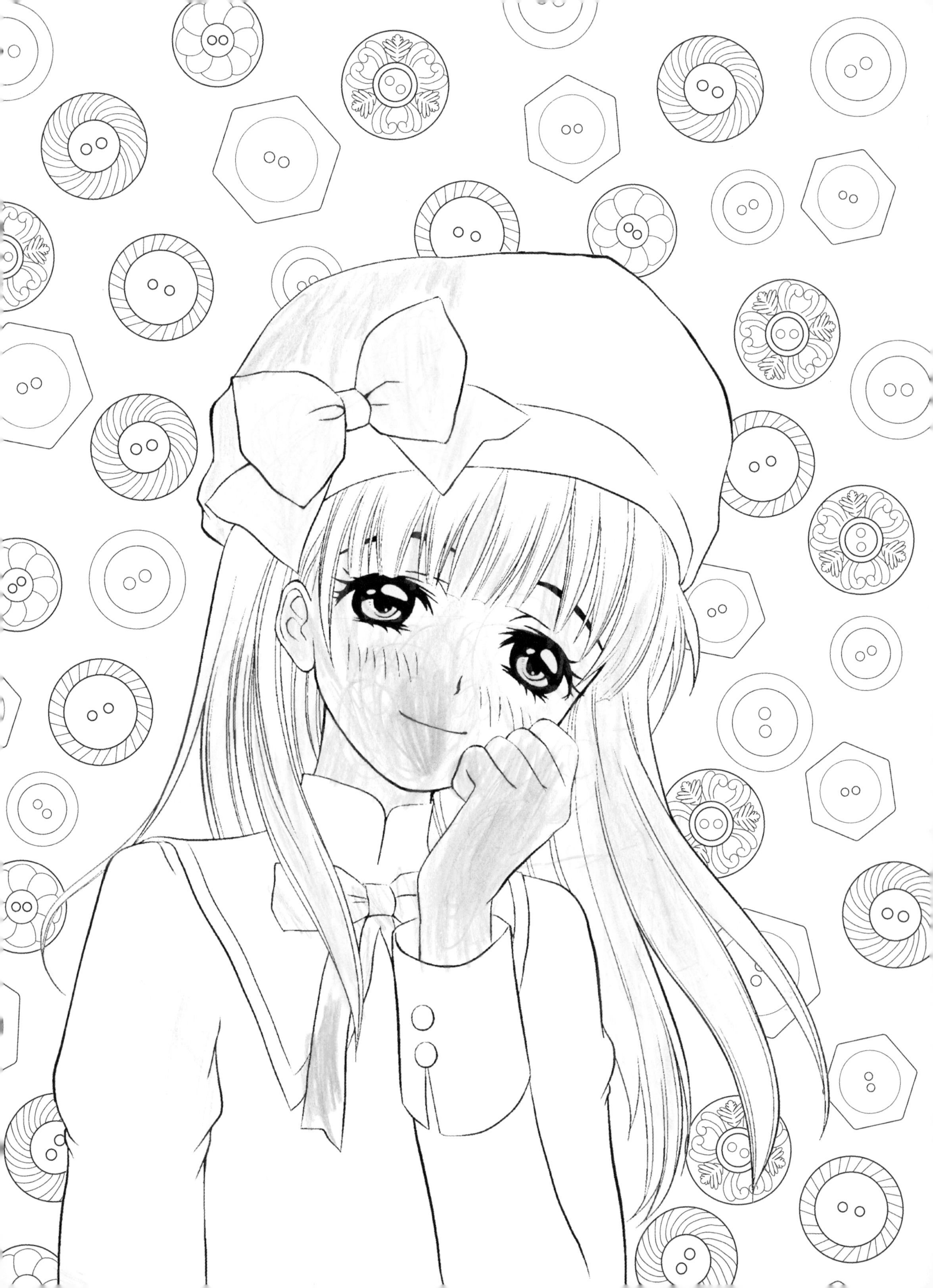

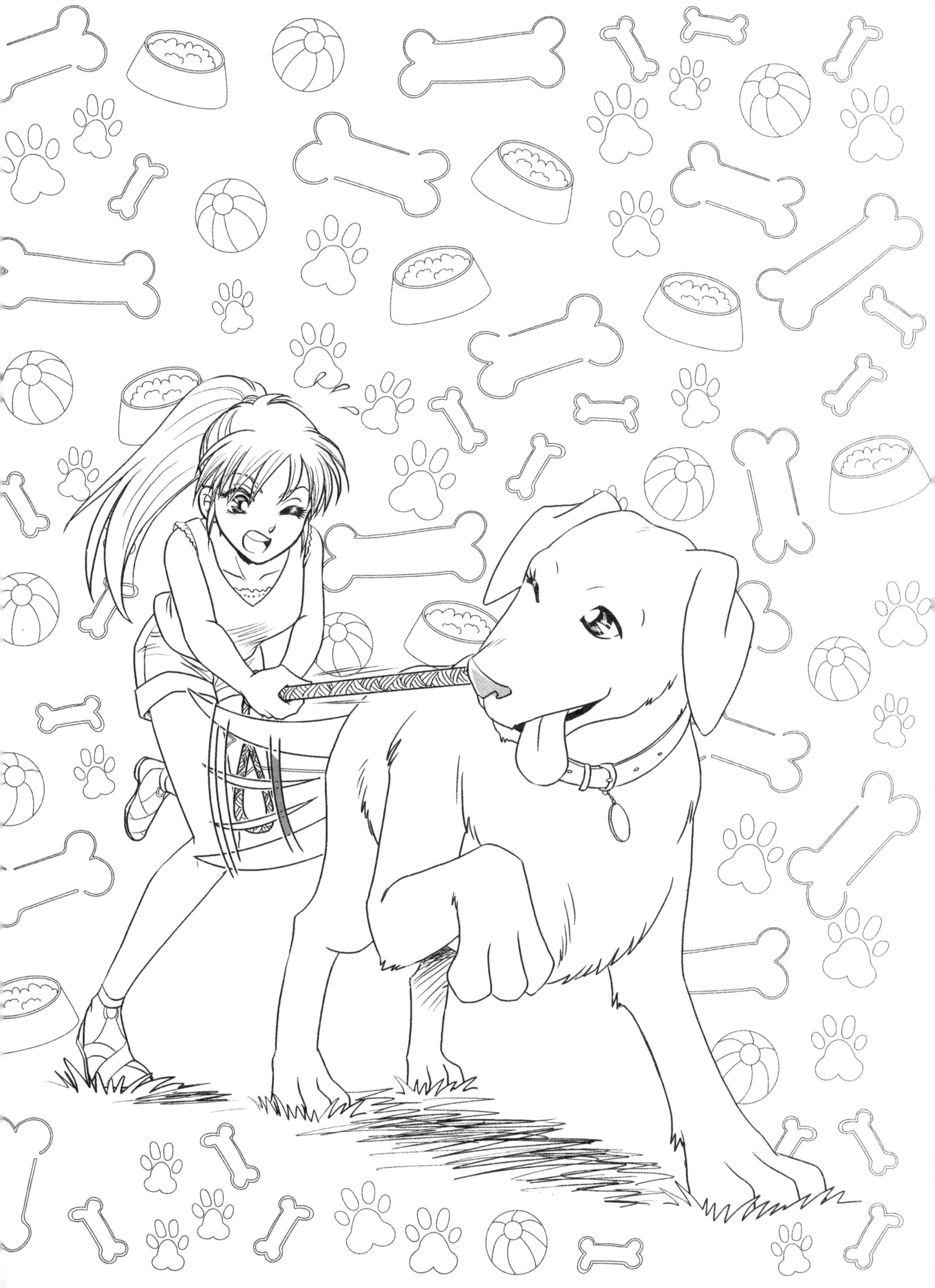

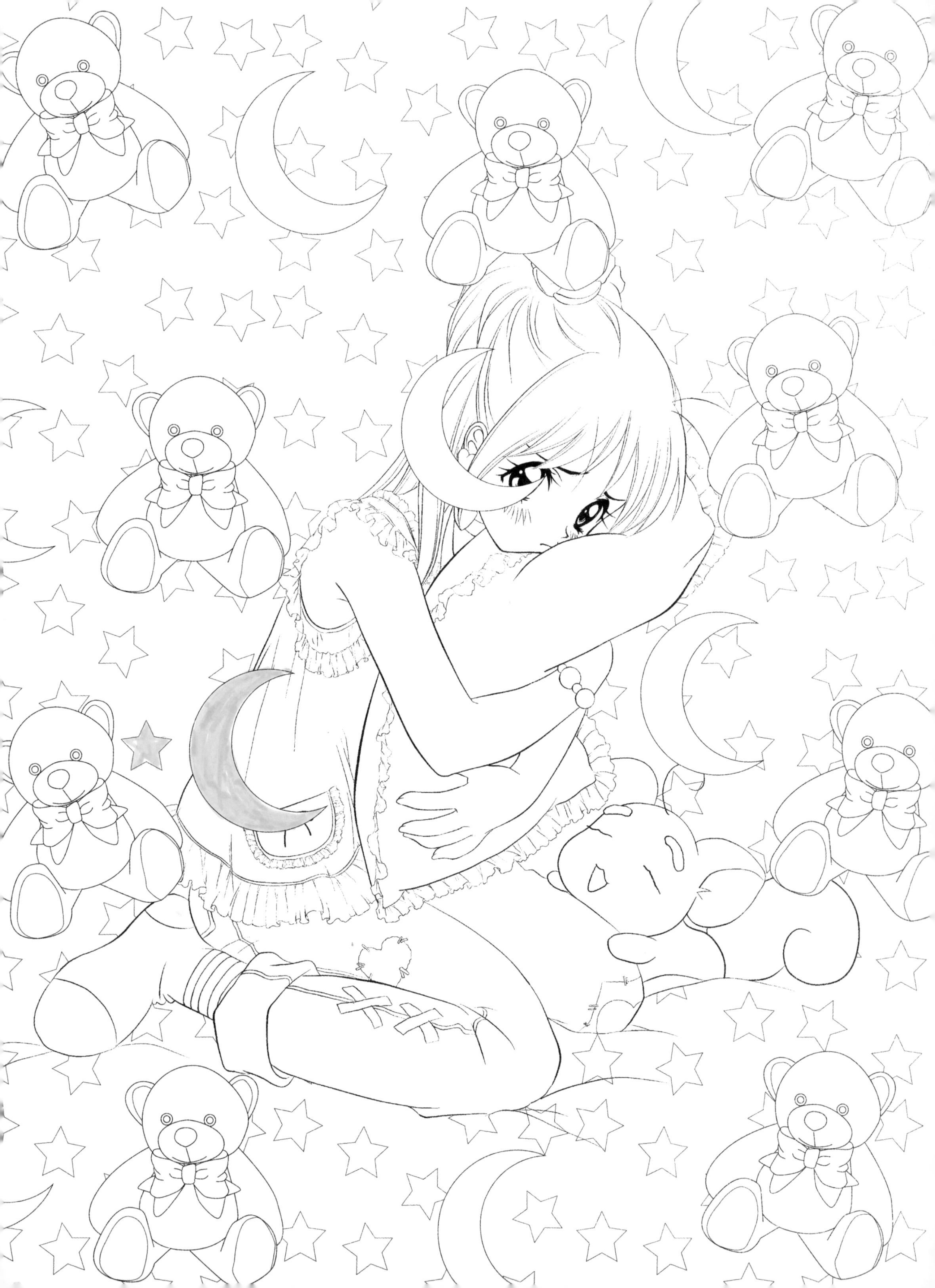

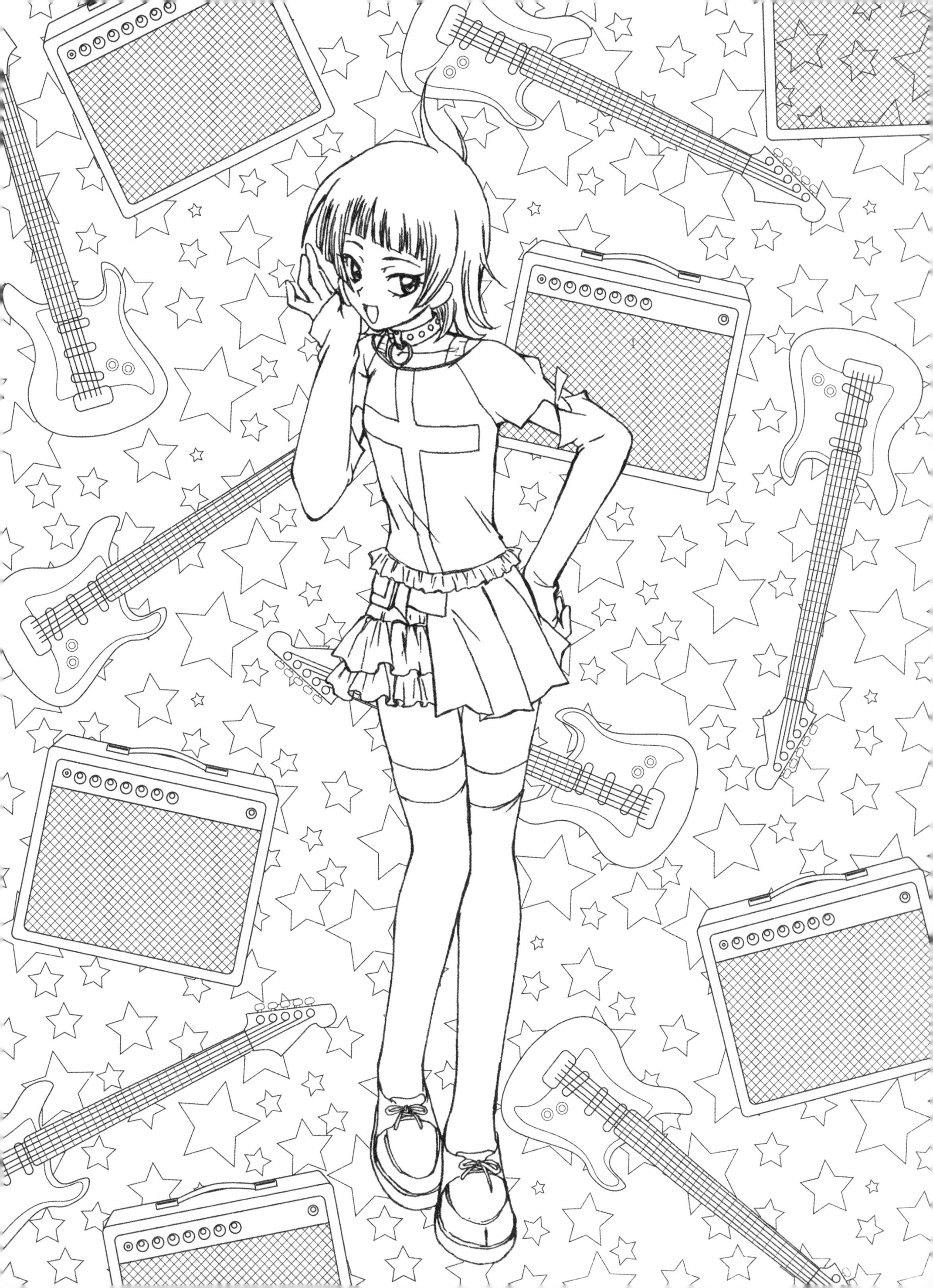

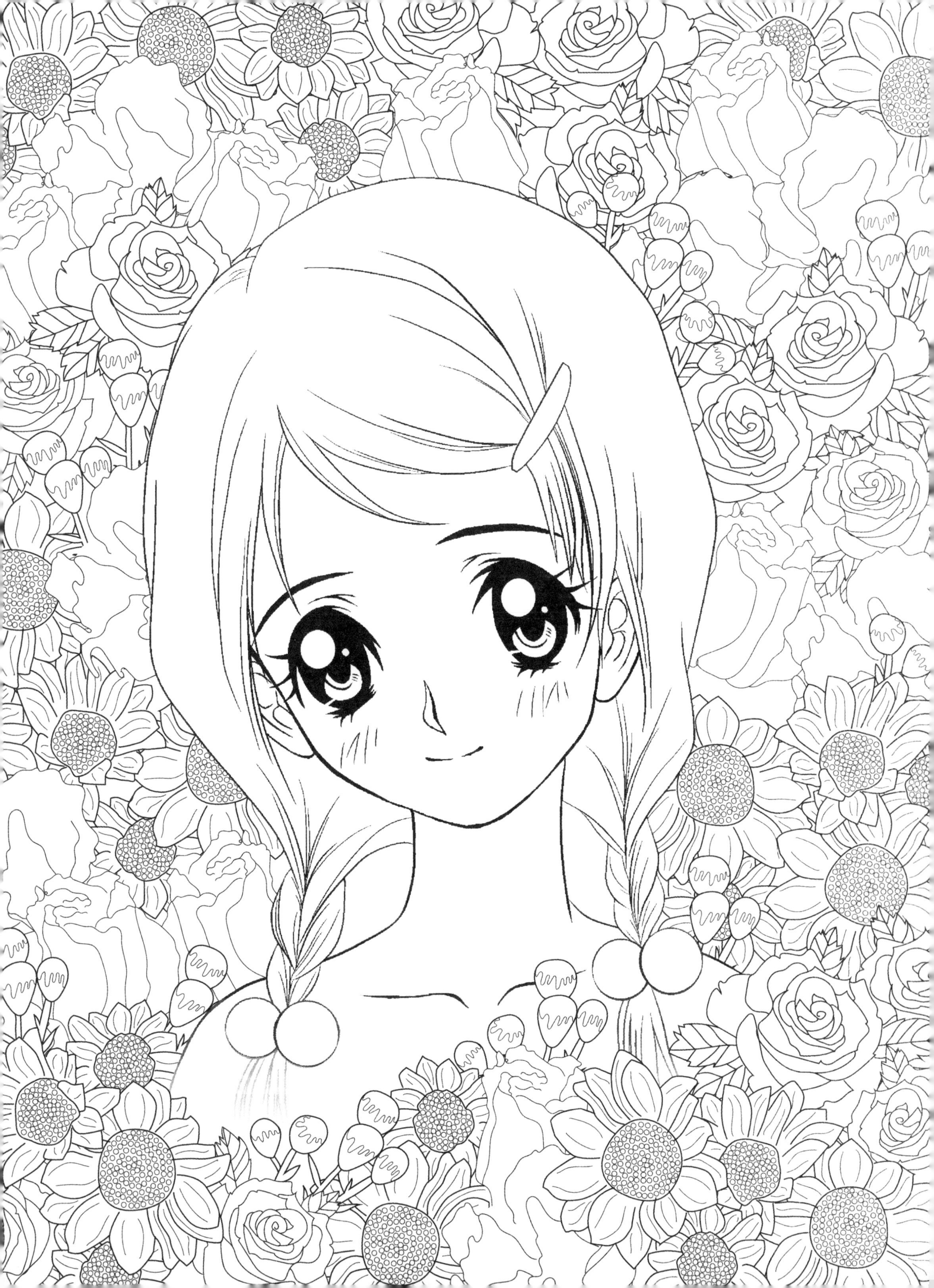

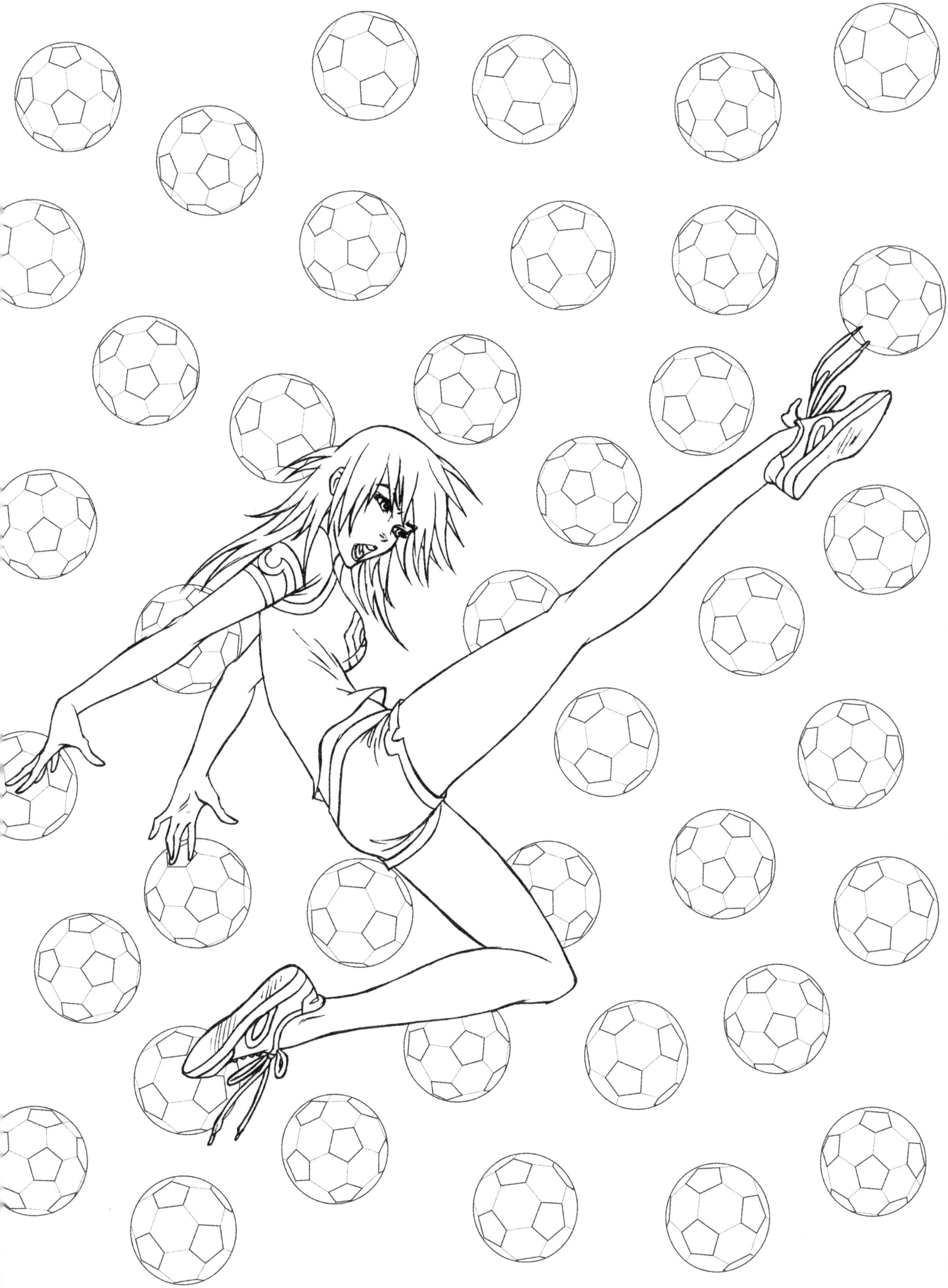

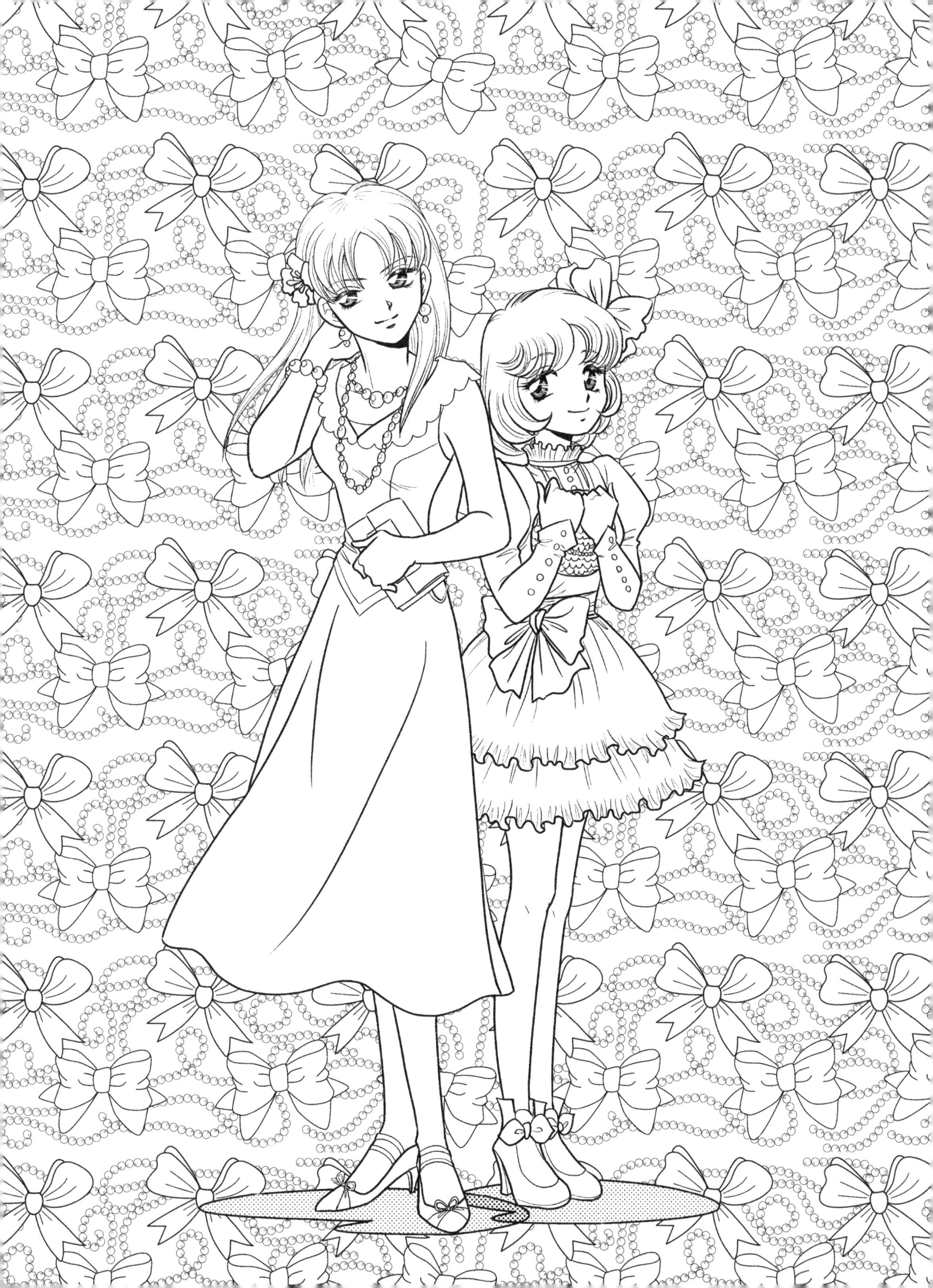

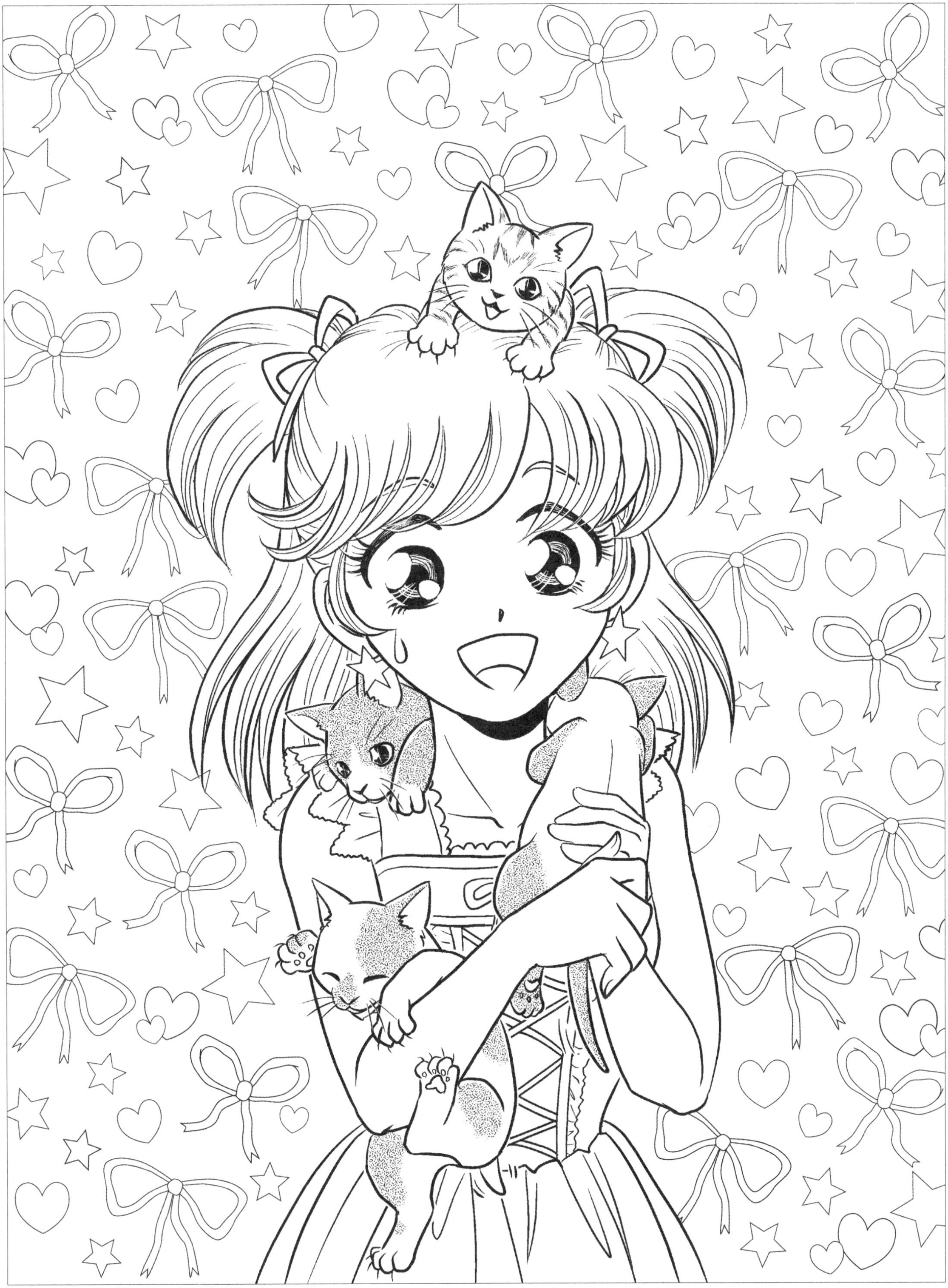

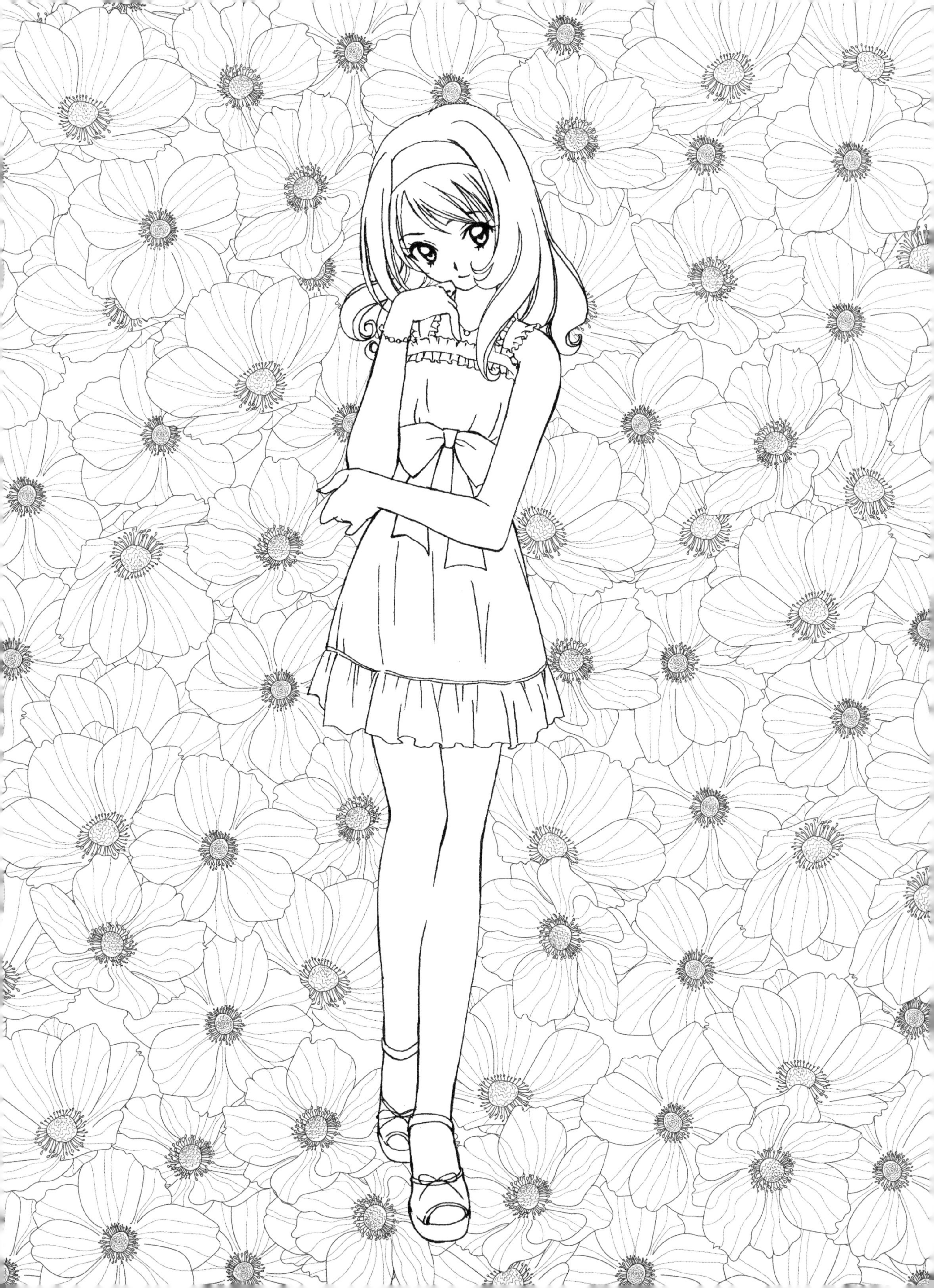

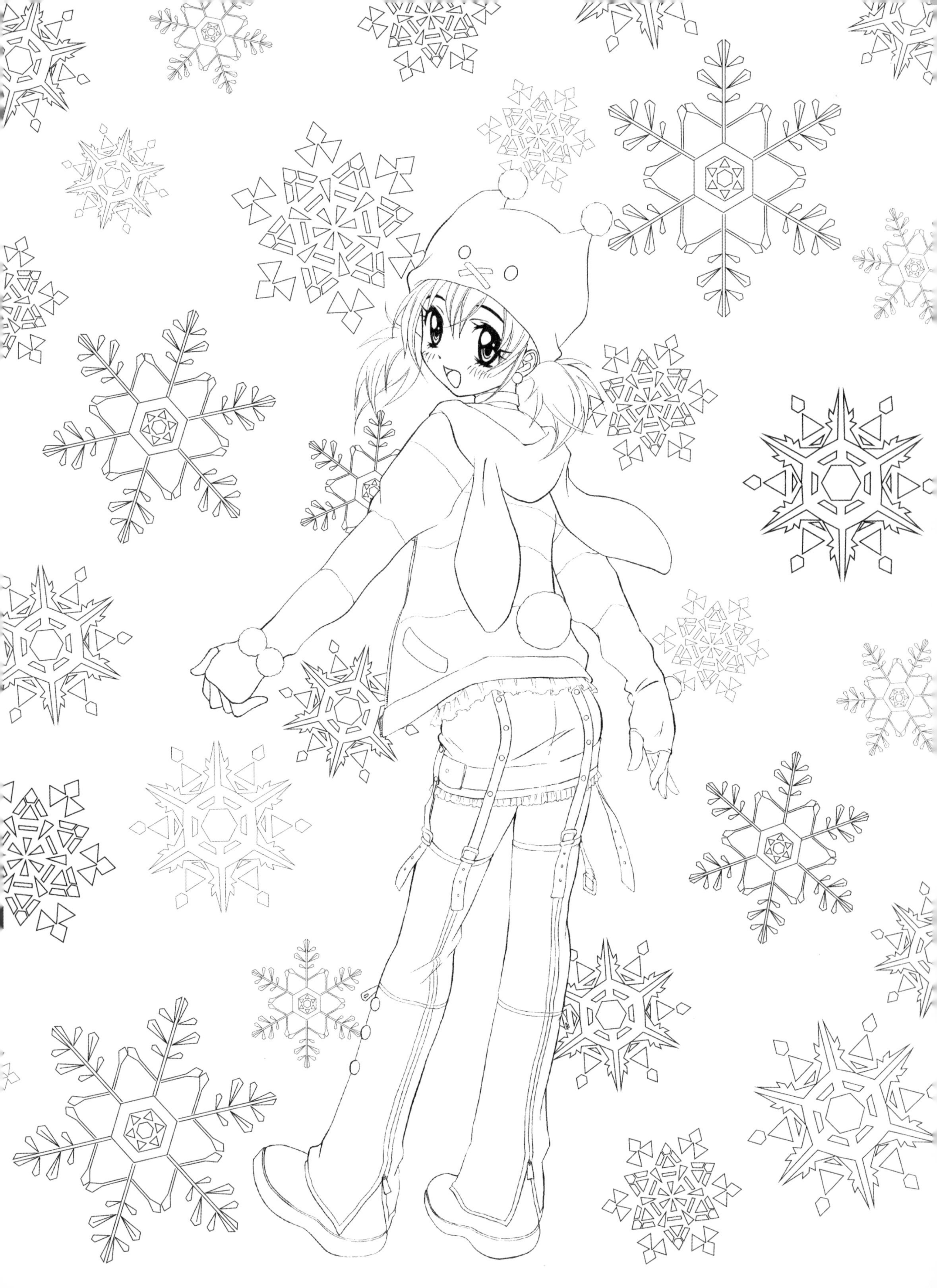

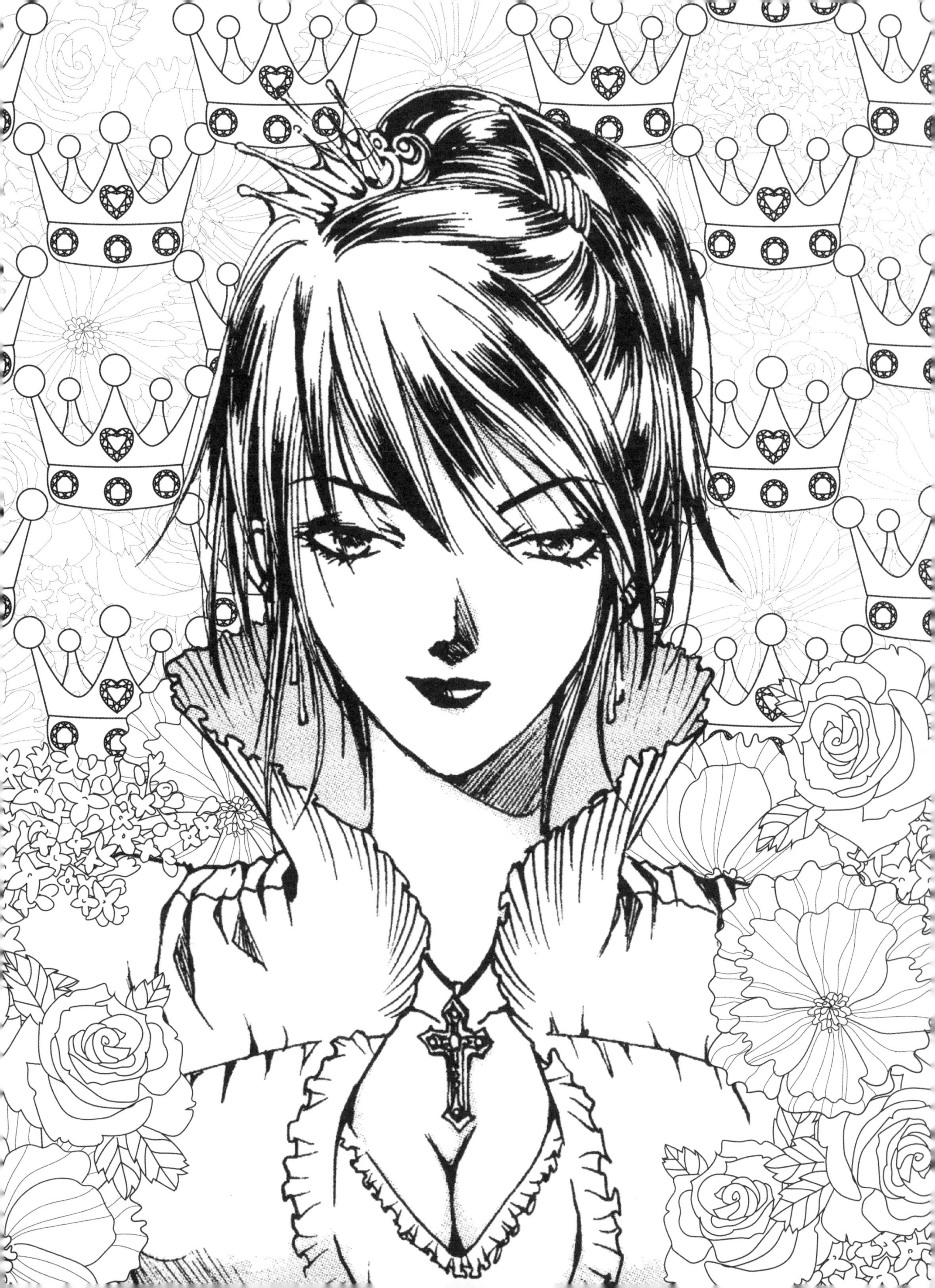

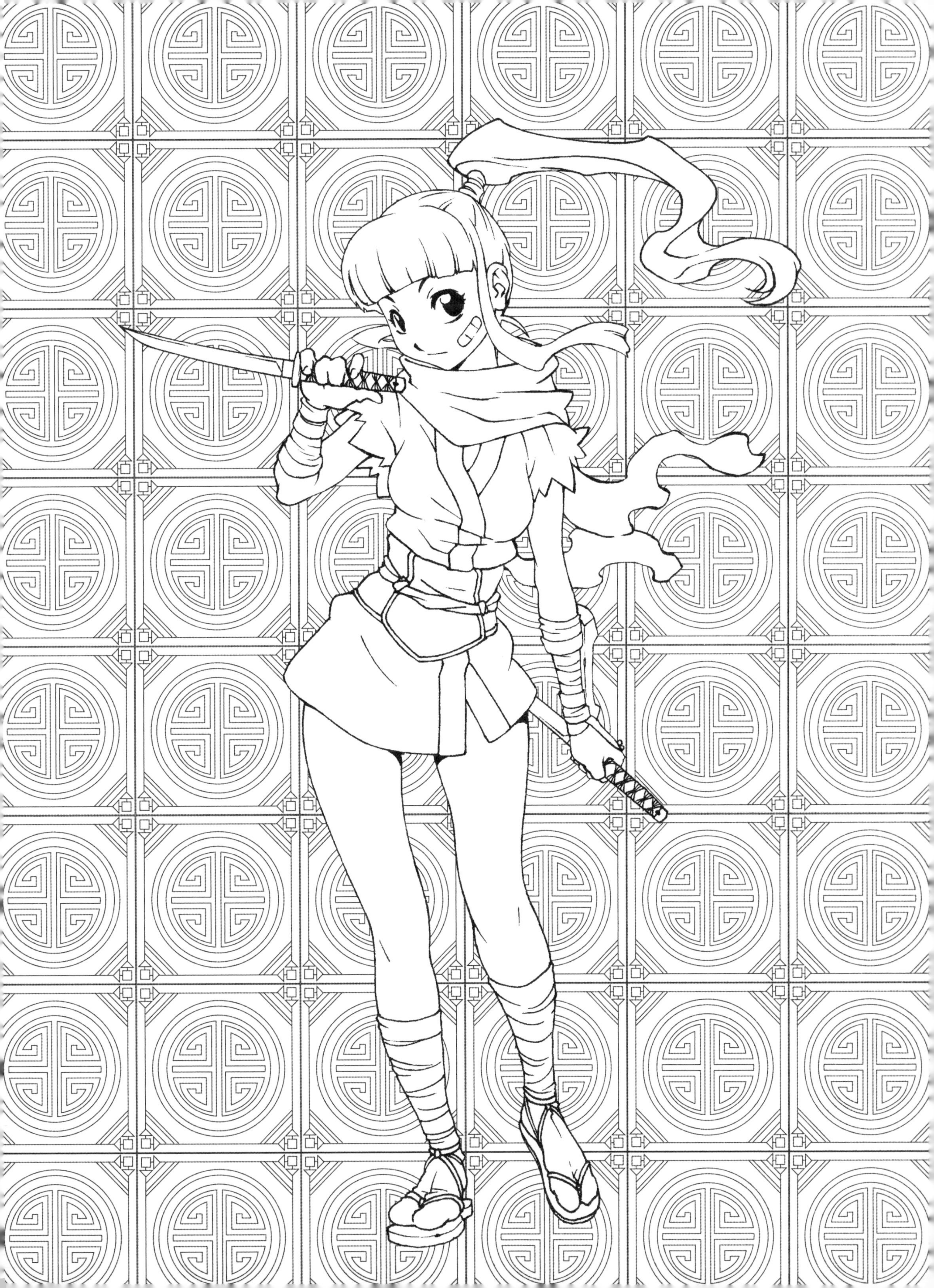

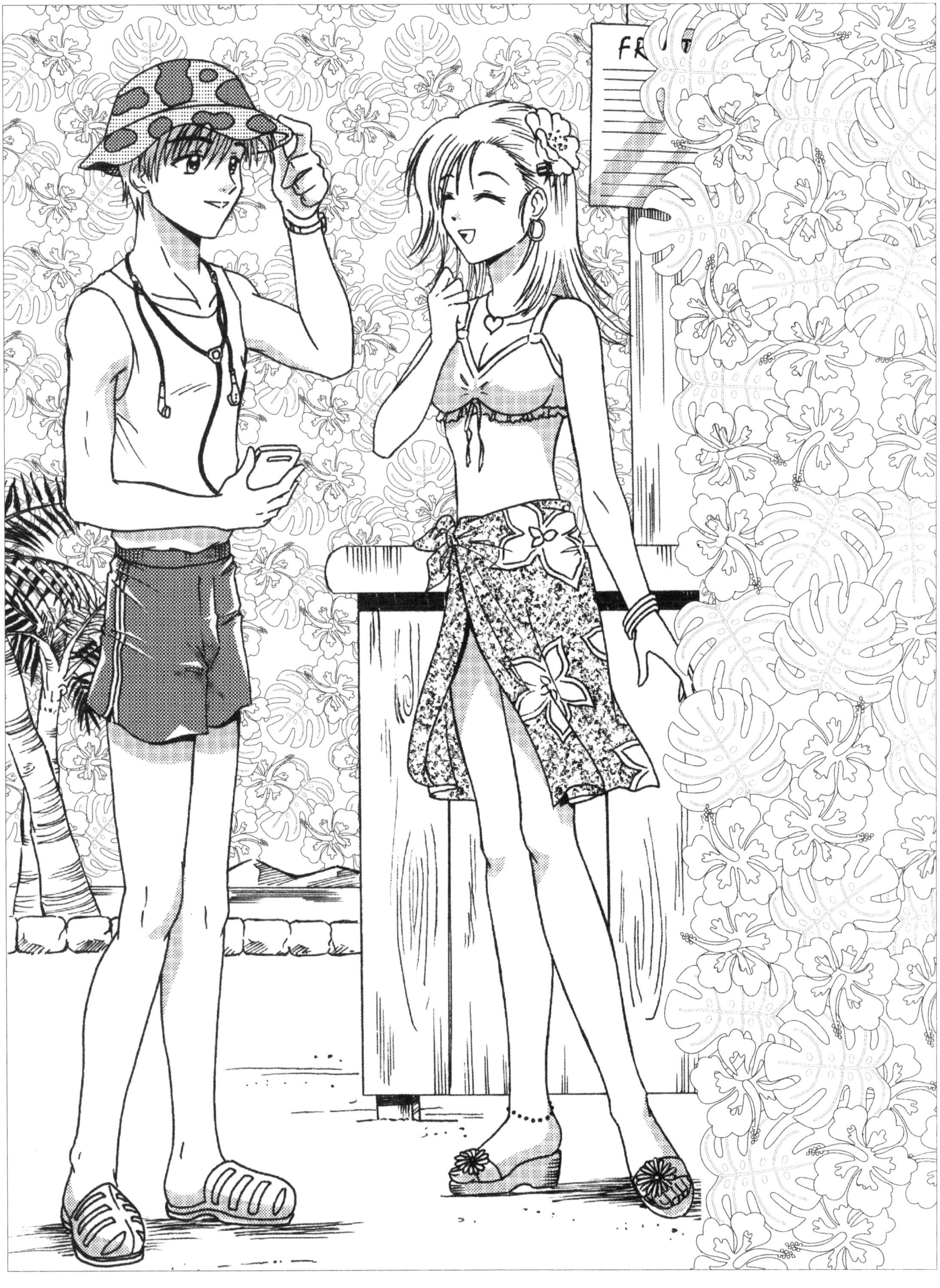

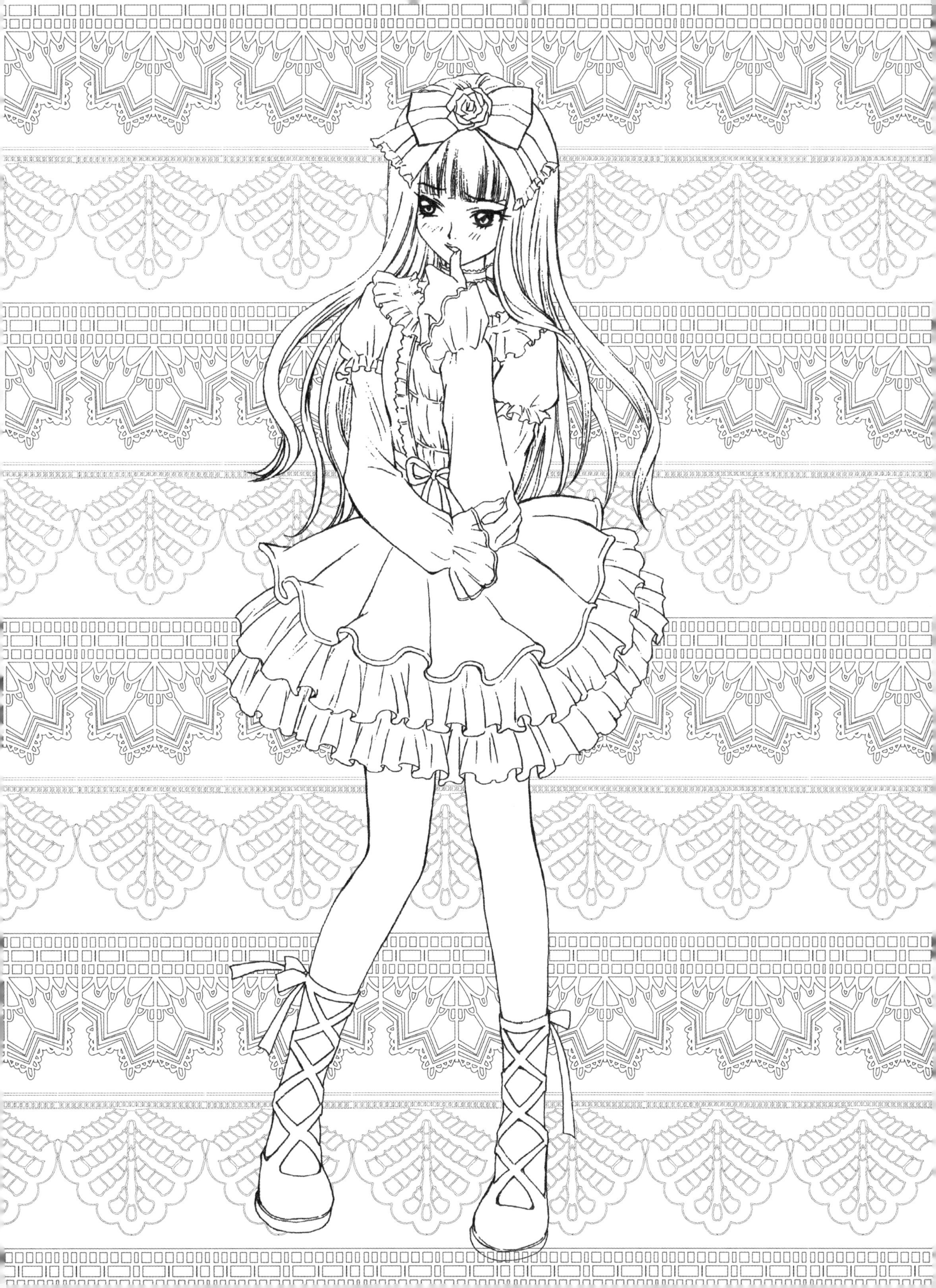

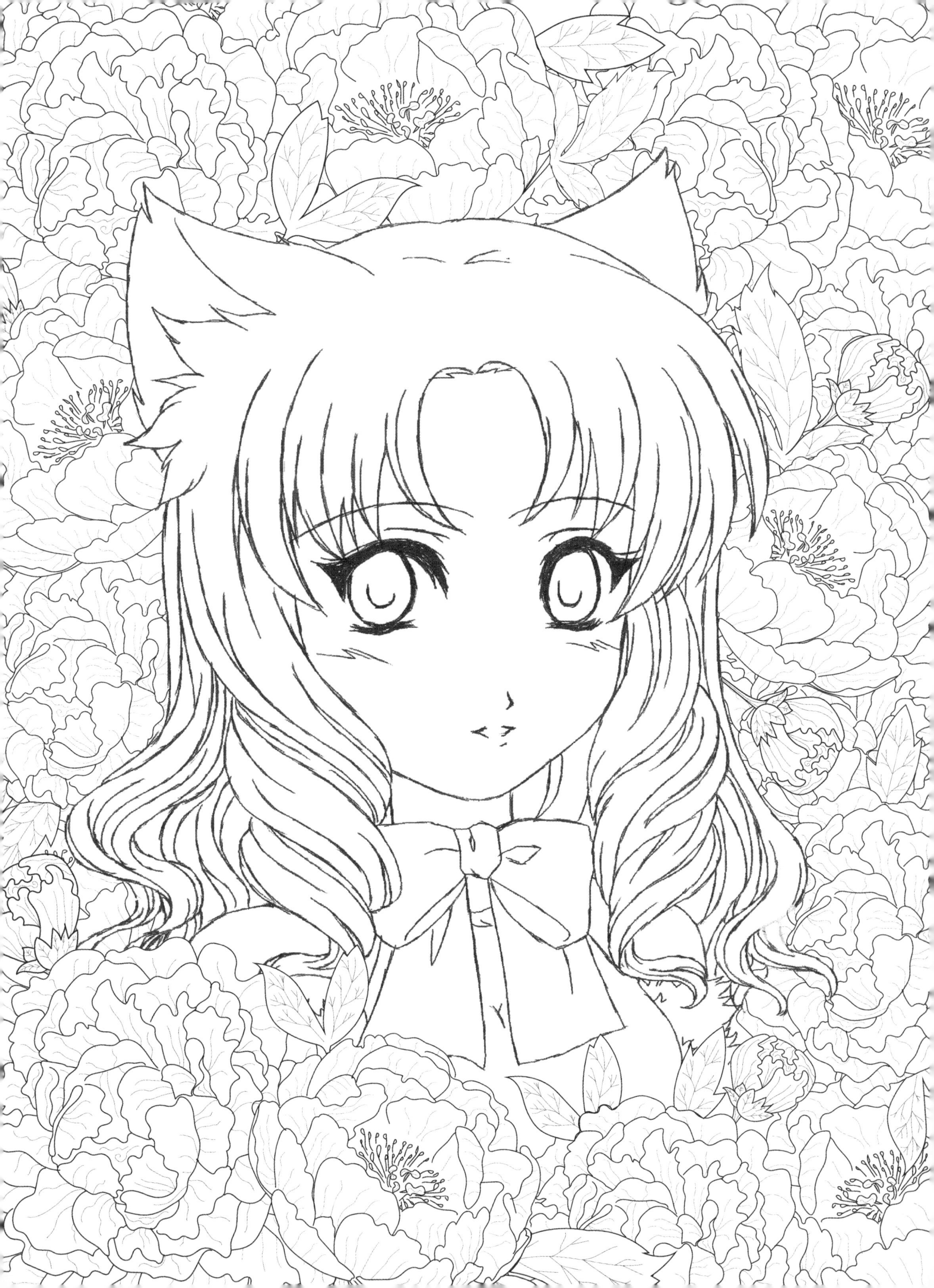

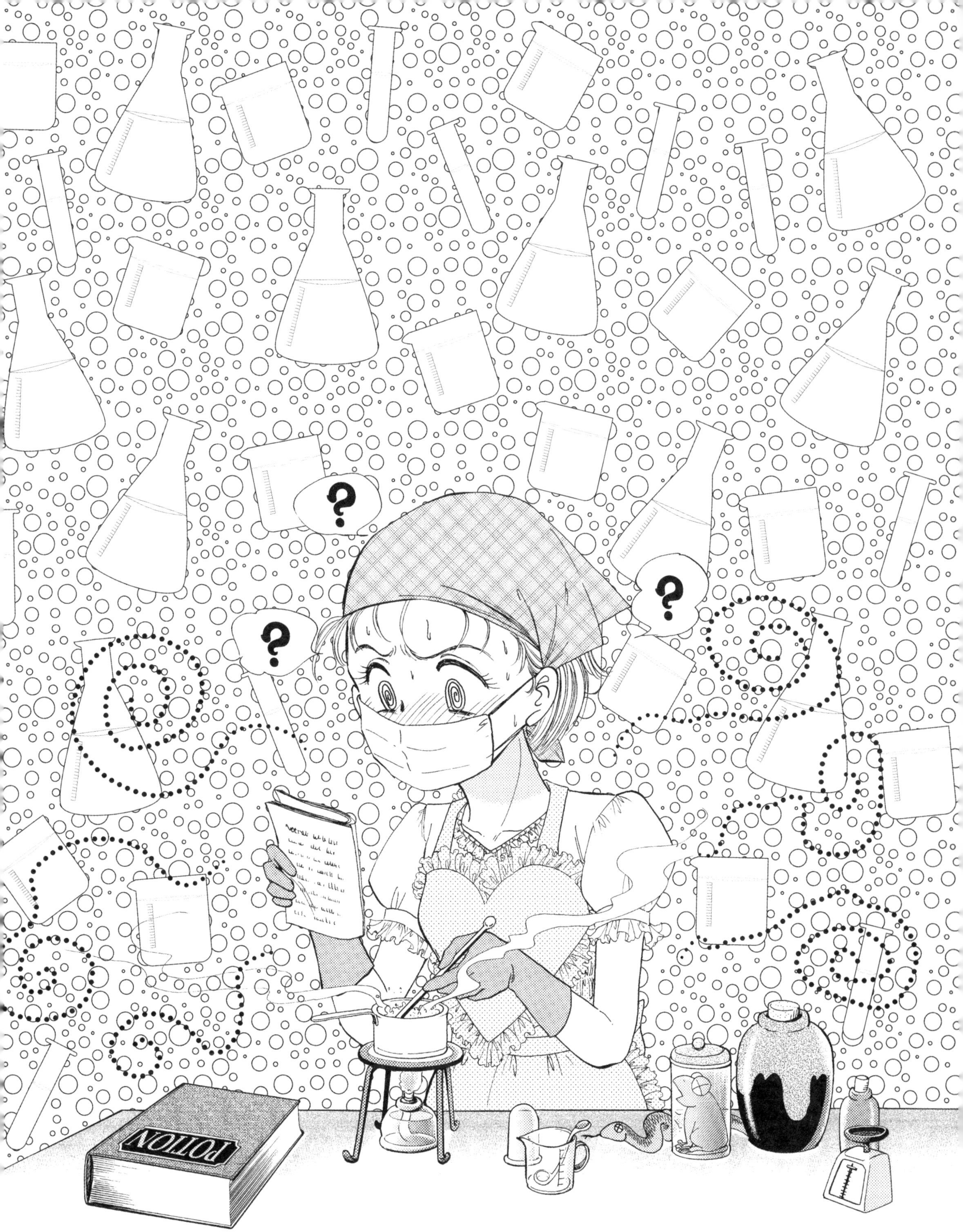
?
?
?
POTION

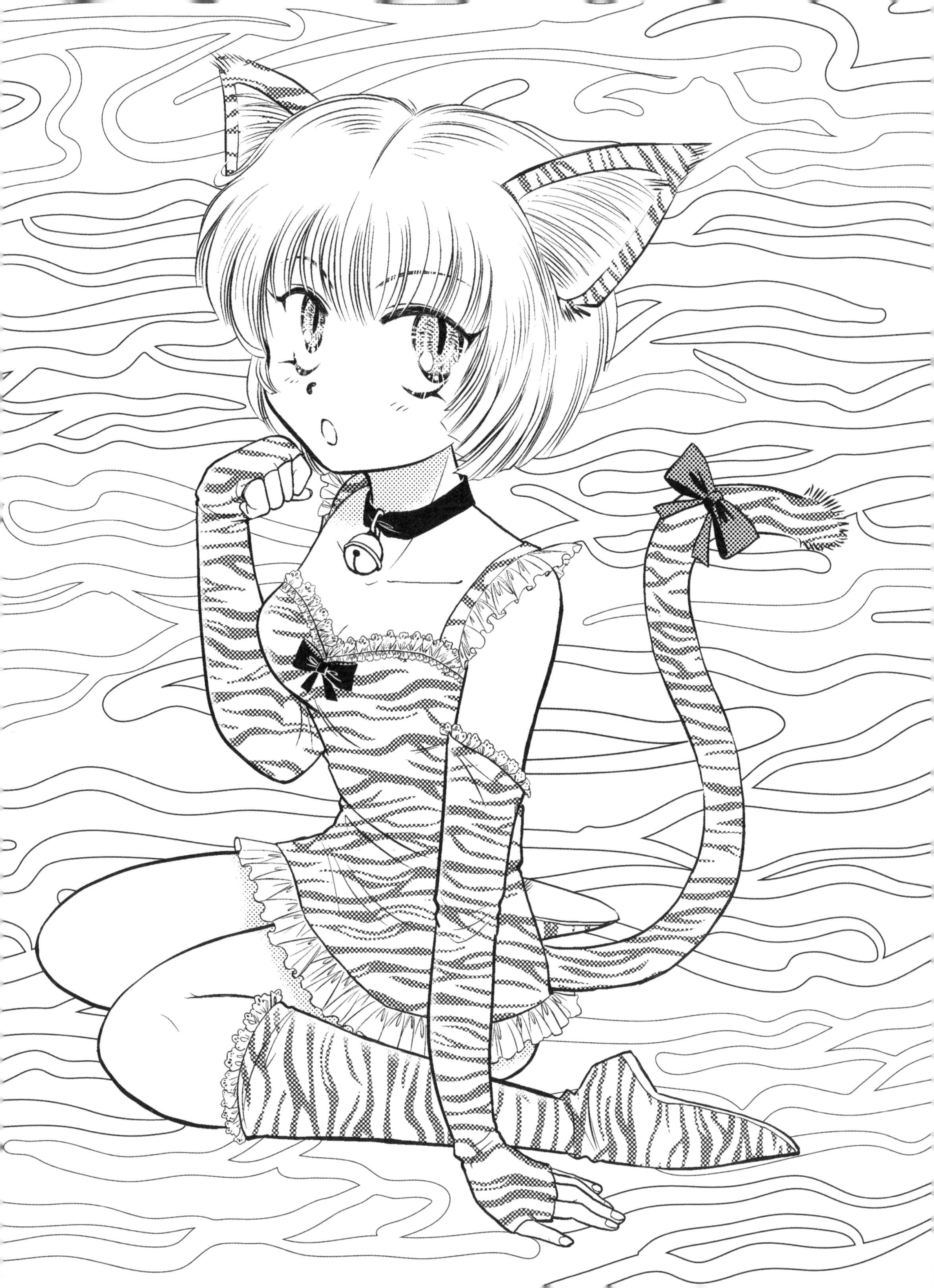

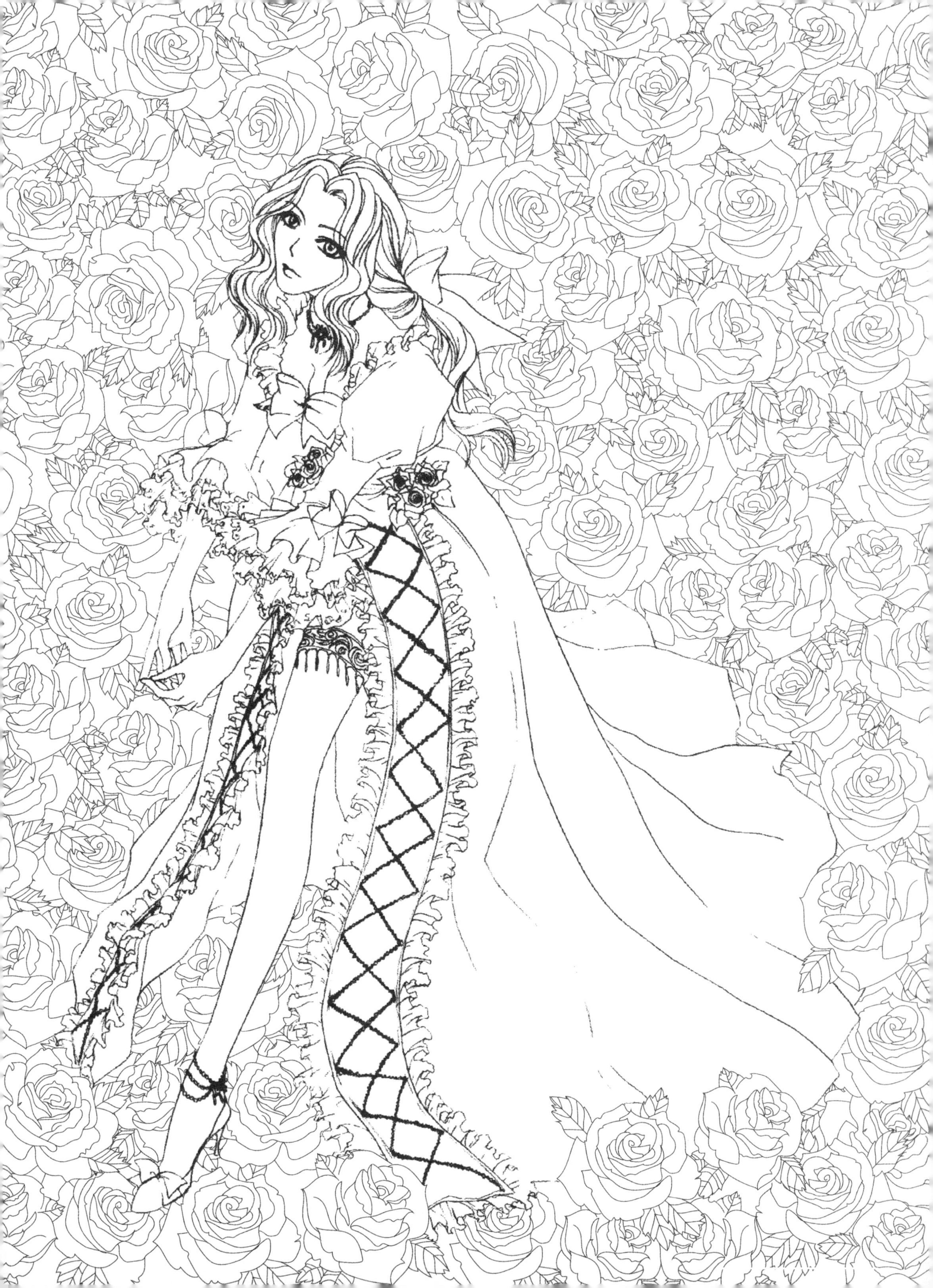

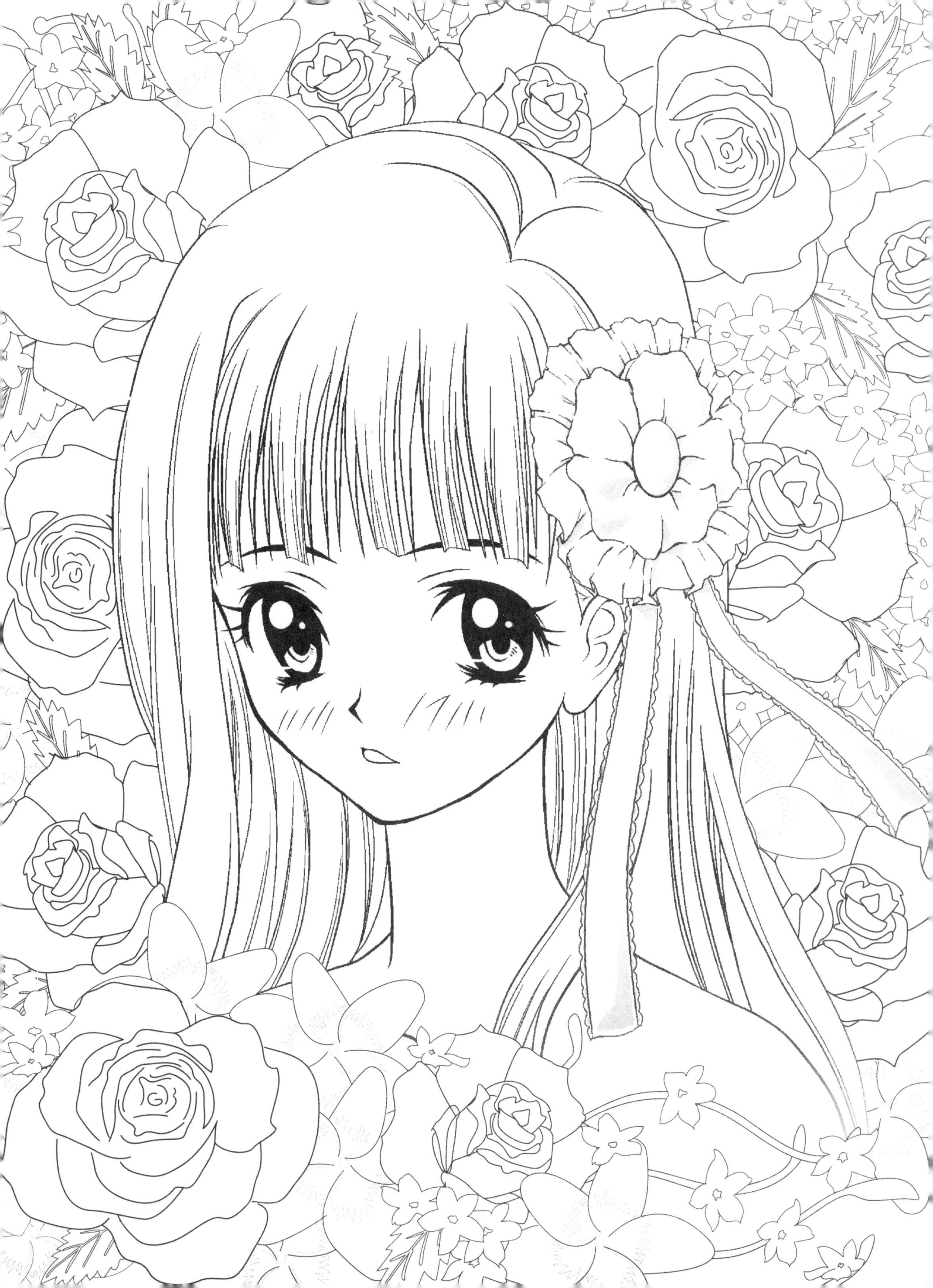

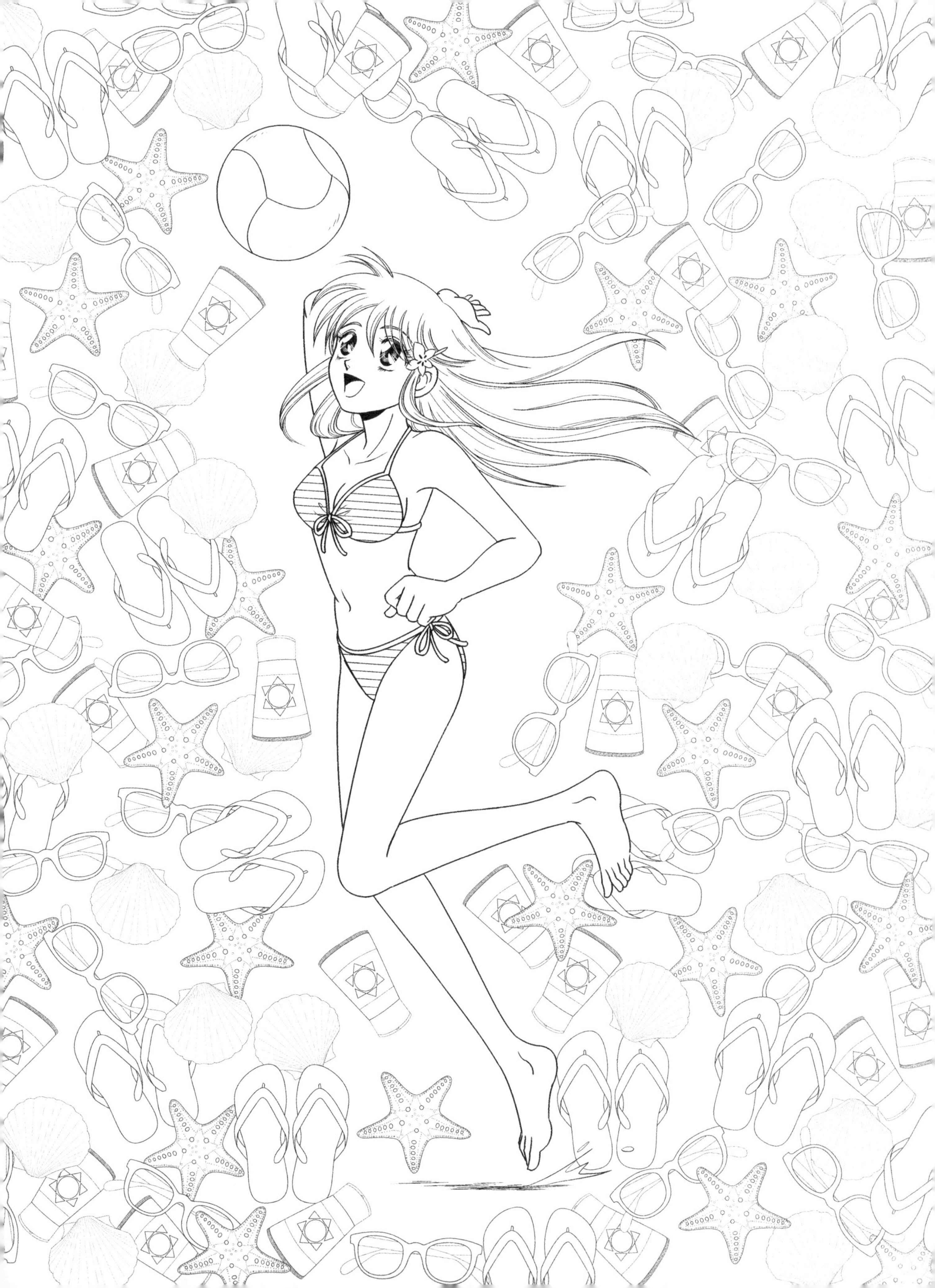

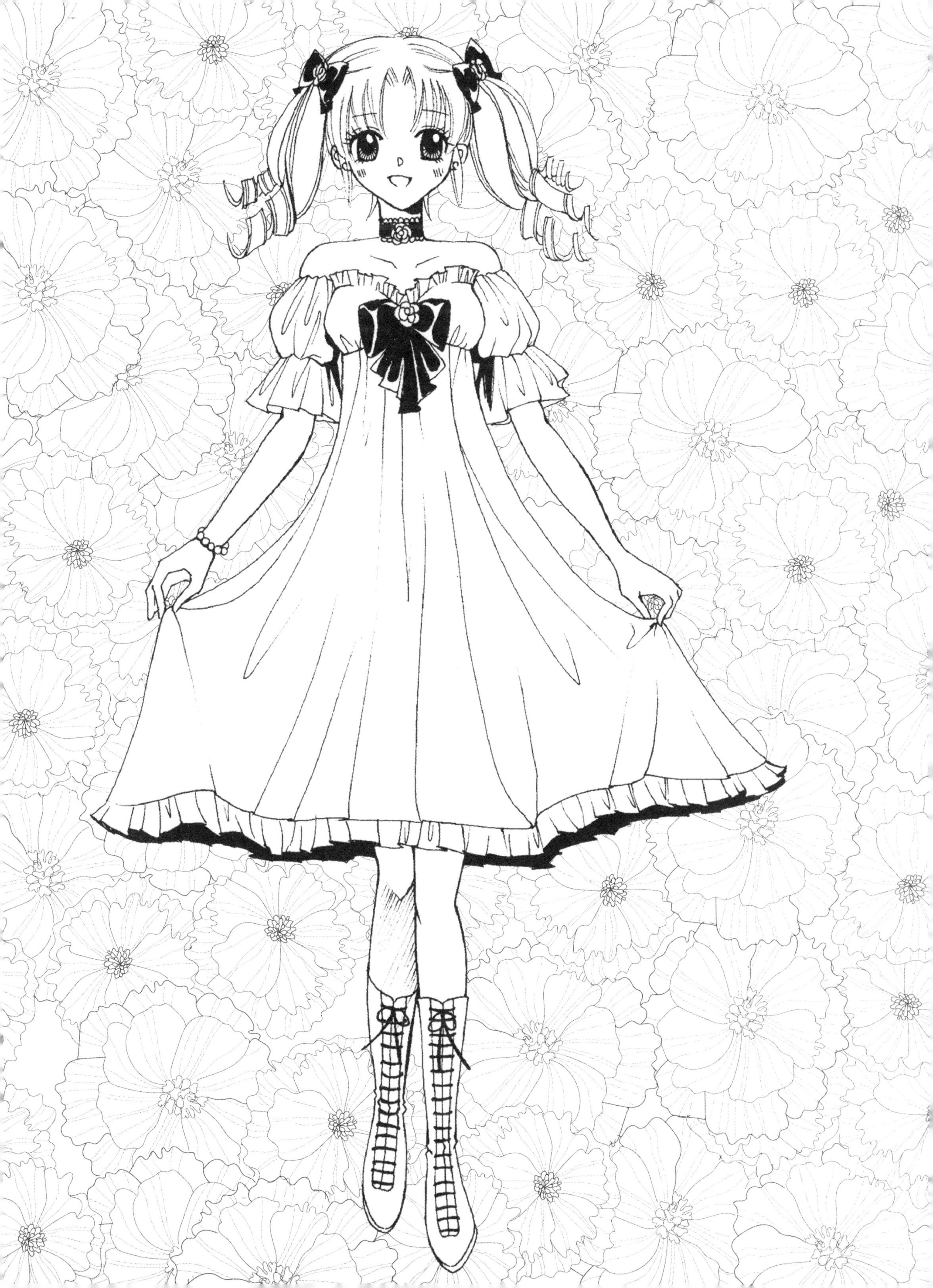

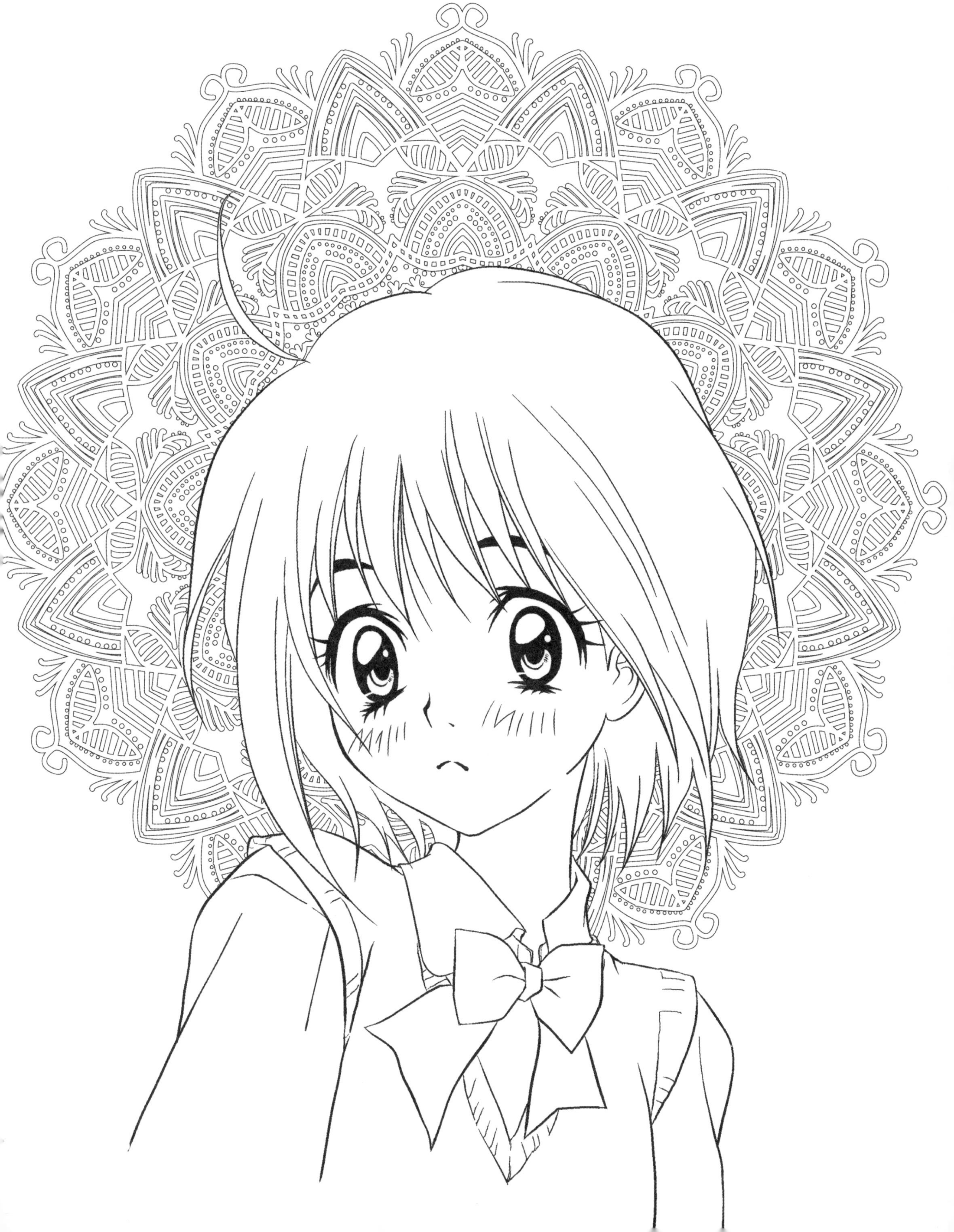

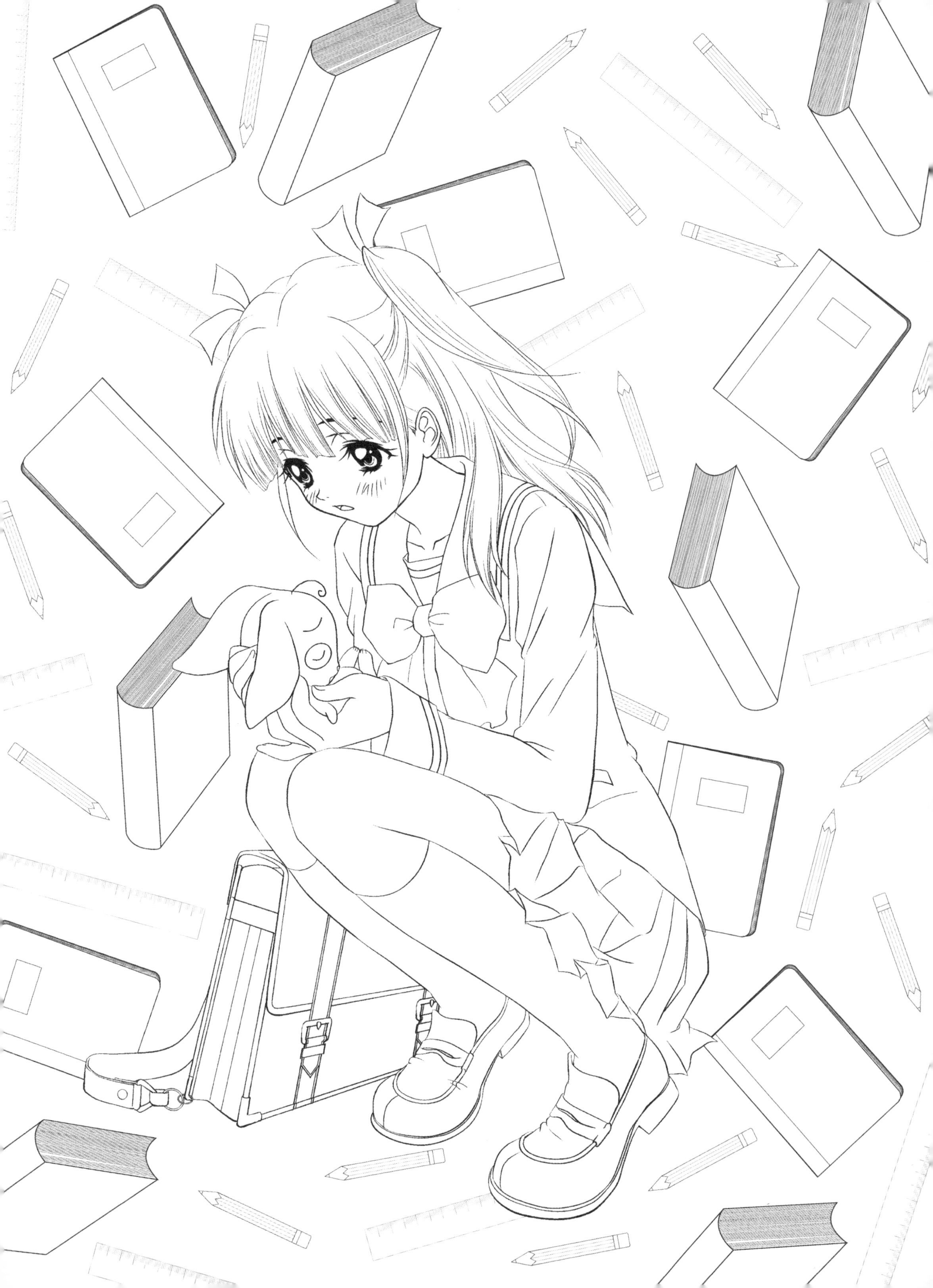

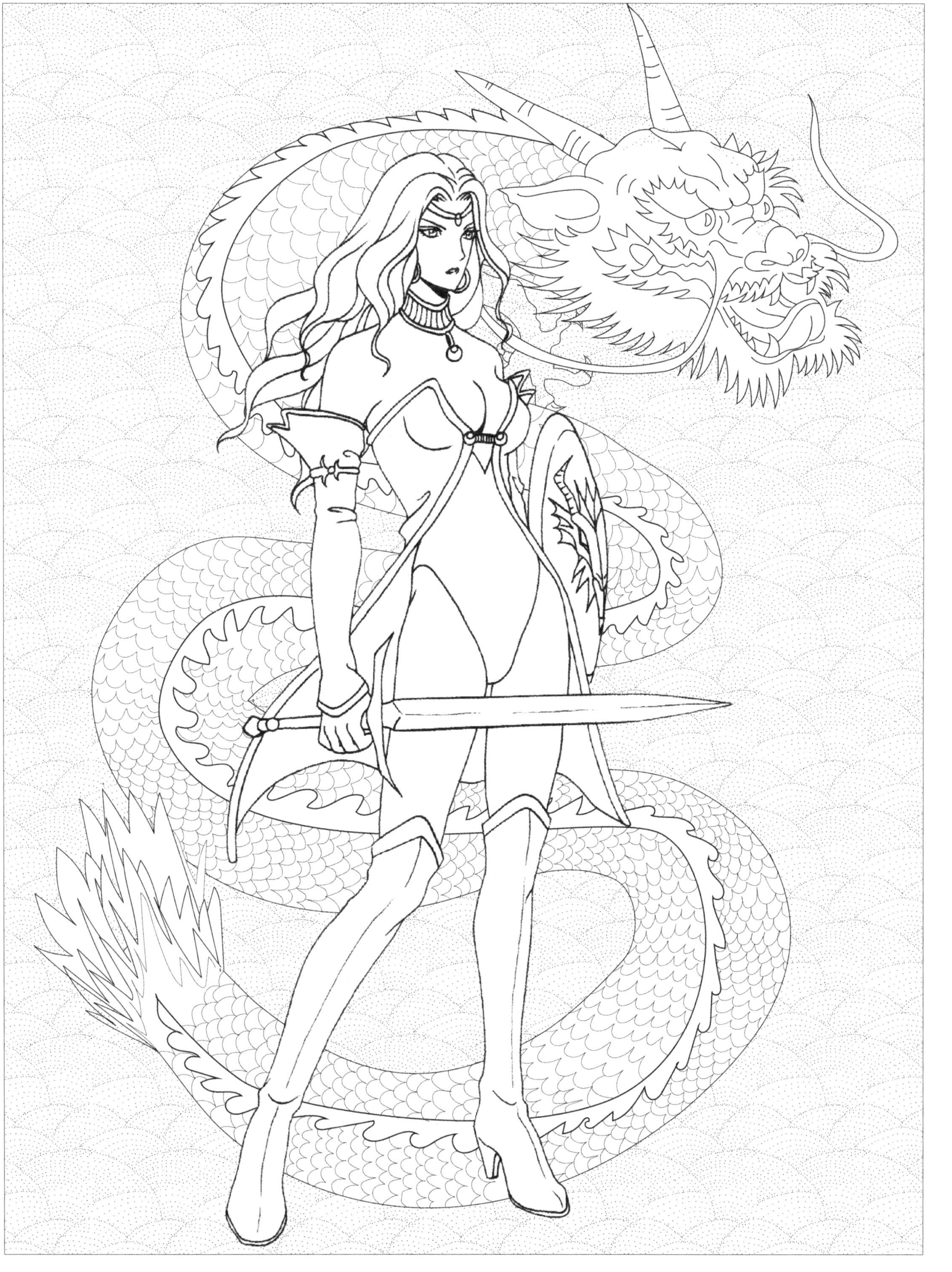

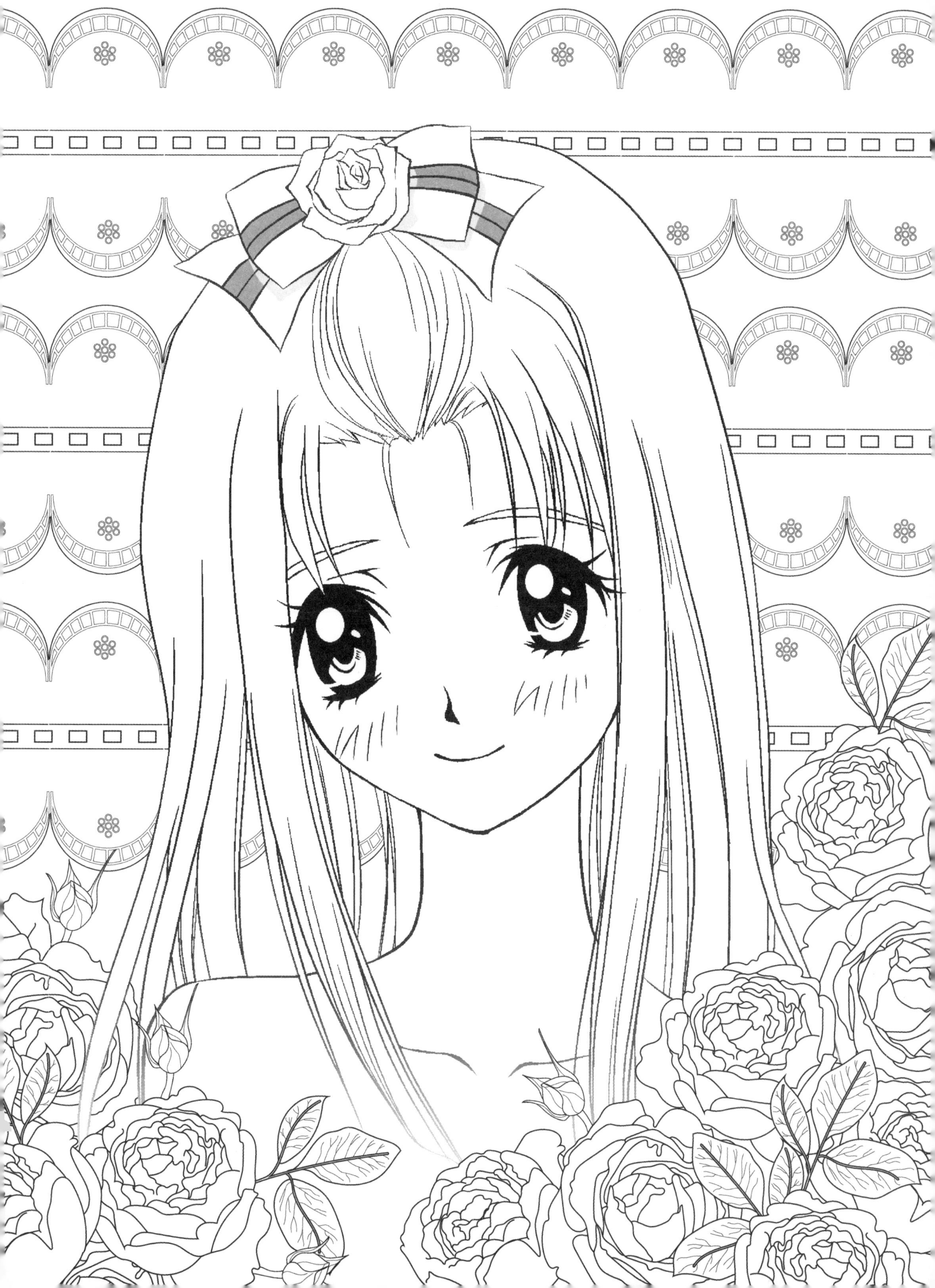